MARVELS OF THE MIND

MARVELS & MYSTERIES

MARVELS OF THE MIND

•PARRALLEL•

CONTENTS

INTRODUCTION

This is a book about the brain and the mind, and the connections between them. Though scientists can tell us a good deal about the way our brains are constructed — the chemical and electrical events that take place there and how it all works — our minds remain a great and marvellous mystery, whose limits and powers are little known and even less understood.

As well as providing information on the way our brains are put together, this book examines the way our minds work by asking some important, and some unusual questions. What is the connection between dreams, the unconscious mind, and our everyday lives? How does hypnotism work, and can it make us more than we are? Is it possible to have more than one mind inhabiting the same body? Do identical twins share a single mind? Is it possible to read what someone else is thinking, or to plant thoughts in someone else's mind? What, exactly, is the difference between fantasy and reality? Should we really learn to expect coincidences? Is there any basis to the belief that certain people can harm others over distances of space and time, by using the power of a curse? Can a whole nation be conquered by the mental powers of a few gifted individuals? Do dumb animals have more brain power than we credit them with? And can we really believe the evidence of our senses?

Also included are the stories of people who have developed and trained their mental abilities so that they can experience and demonstrate marvellous powers, people who feel no pain while walking barefoot on flaming coals, people who can make important scientific discoveries through clairvoyance and even people who can move around the world whilst leaving their bodies at home.

THE UNCONSCIOUS STOREHOUSE

MANY PEOPLE HAVE A FANTASTIC ABILITY TO DISCUSS THEIR PAST LIVES IN VIVID DETAIL — BUT ALL TOO OFTEN IT TURNS OUT THEY ARE RECITING SOMETHING ONCE READ OR HEARD

The subconscious mind can be regarded as a vast, muddled storehouse of information. This information comes from books, newspapers and magazines; from lectures, television and radio; from direct observation, and from overheard scraps of conversation. In normal circumstances, most of this knowledge is not subject to recall, but there are times when some of these deeply buried memories are spontaneously revived.

Hypnotic regression, seen below, was particularly fashionable in the early years of the century, and is currently enjoying a revival.

And some of these revived memories re-emerge as baffling examples of cryptomnesia – memories with origins that have been completely forgotten.

As a result, material can sometimes seem to have no ancestry and can be mistaken for something newly discovered or created. The late Helen Keller – blind, deaf and mute from infancy – was tragically deceived by such a cryptomnesiac caprice. In 1892, she wrote a charming tale called *The Frost King*. It was published and applauded; but within a few months, it was revealed that the piece was simply a modified version of Margaret Canby's story *The Frost Fairies*, published 29 years earlier. Helen had no conscious memory of ever having heard the story, but it was established that a friend had read a batch of Miss Canby's stories to her in 1888 – and *The Frost Fairies* was among them. Helen Keller was devastated. She wrote:

'Joy deserted my heart... I had disgraced myself... yet how could it possibly have happened? I racked my brain until I was weary to recall anything about the frost that I had read before I wrote *The Frost King,* but I could remember nothing.'

In the same fashion, a number of cases of automatic writings – allegedly from discarnate spirits – have been traced to published works. For example, the famous 'Oscar Wilde' scripts, produced by two

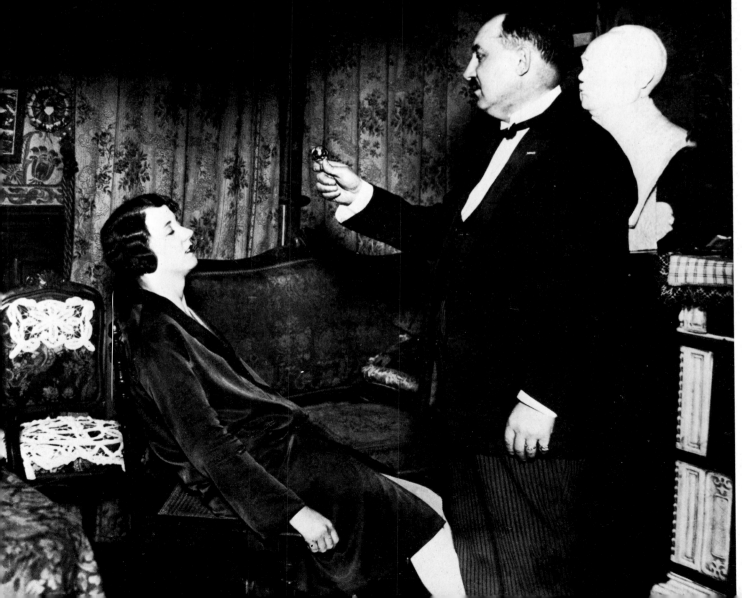

Later research seemed to show, however, that Hélène's obscure Indian knowledge was drawn from an inaccurate history by De Marles, published in 1823, and that she ' ... dug down to the very bottom of her memories without discovering the slightest traces of this work'. However, the real proof of her ability to resurrect and restructure unconscious knowledge came with her most extravagant romance – one involving contact with the inhabitants of Mars.

During her Martian episode, Hélène produced a small album of exotic drawings of Martian landscapes, houses, people and plants. But these were all typically childish fantasies with superficial oriental touches. Much more impressive was the emergence of a spoken and written Martian language. Yet an analysis of 'Martian' showed that the sounds were those of the French language; the order of words was absolutely the same as in French, and its crude grammar was simply a parody of that of her mother tongue. The vocabulary alone was her

psychics in the 1920s, were shown to be derived from many printed sources, including Wilde's own *De Profundis* and *The Decay of Lying*. One of the writers of the automatic scripts, Dr S.G. Soal, was led to remark: 'The variety of sources from which the script is drawn is as amazing as the adroitness with which the knowledge is worked up into sentences conveying impressions of the different mannerisms of Wilde's literary style.' This is a significant verdict indeed, for very often the cryptomnesic material emerges not in a pure form, but in an edited or paraphrased version. And this may mislead investigators in search of primary sources.

SOUND EVIDENCE?

Such unconscious plagiarisms are certainly intriguing, but most baffling of all are surely the vivid memories of 'past lives' that emerge under hypnosis or trance conditions. To some, these have always smacked of cryptomnesia; but to many others, this explanation seems ruled out by the great wealth of detail – often obscure – provided by such 'regressionists'. Here, the use of tape recorders has proved invaluable. Before their introduction, all such research was costly and time-consuming, since everything the subject said had to be taken down in shorthand with the inevitable loss of any accents, nuances and subtleties in the voice. Sound tapes, by contrast, seem to provide lively and more convincing case records than any of those furnished by the pioneer researchers. Even so, there are two classic cases from the turn of the century that still command respect. The most famous involved the Swiss medium, Hélène Smith.

Hélène was investigated by Theodore Flournoy, professor of psychology at Geneva University. He published his major findings in *From India to the Planet Mars*. In this book, he records that Hélène laid claim to a previous existence as the ill-fated Queen of France, Marie-Antoinette. She also claimed a much earlier reincarnation as the wife of the Hindu prince Sivrouka Nayaka, a 15th-century ruler of Kanara, India. Her Indian memories were enriched with descriptions of ceremonies and palaces, but complicated by her insistence that Flournoy had also been present in Kanara – as her husband!

that the facts were drawn from an historical novel. Miss C. could recall reading only one novel set in that period: *John Standish*. But this did not feature the material in Blanche's messages.

Further research by Lowes Dickinson only increased his bewilderment. More and more facts came to light that confirmed Blanche's story, but some were drawn from such obscure genealogical data that he began to feel that they would never have been incorporated in a novel. For a while, he came to 'think it possible that Miss C. was really communicating with the departed Blanche Poynings.'

The first stage of a solution to the mystery came at a tea party at Miss C.'s house. Her aunt and brother were present and began talking about the then current craze for planchette readings. (The planchette is a small board supported on castors

Swiss medium Hélène Smith claimed to have contacted Martians. She drew one of them, Astane, left, his house, above left, and his 'ugly beast', below, whose body is covered with pink hair, and who has a black head and a green eye.

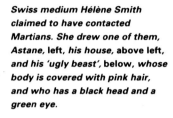

invention. Even so, the whole affair involved a remarkable feat of construction and memory, for Hélène was always consistent in her use of what she believed to be 'Martian'. All this was apparently the work of her subconscious.

Although not everyone was satisfied by Flournoy's explanation of the Hélène Smith case, the Blanche Poynings case of 1906 was neatly solved within a few months.

Blanche Poynings was a woman who had lived during the reign of Richard II. Ostensibly, she began – in 1906 – to communicate through a clergyman's daughter, known as Miss C., while under hypnosis. Blanche, it seemed, had been a friend of the Countess of Salisbury and proved to be a garrulous gossip. She poured out details of the Countess' affairs, correctly naming her two husbands, children, in-laws and retainers. She also chatted about her own four marriages and her time at court.

A Rich, Detailed Account

Everyday events were not neglected either, for Blanche tattled away – through Miss C. – about the fashion: 'Men wore shoes with long points which were chained to their knees. They had long hair cut straight across the forehead.' And, apparently, she ' ... used to wear brocaded velvet, trimmed with ermine, and a high-peaked cap of miniver'. Among other tit-bits was mention of the three types of bread eaten by the different classes – namely, simmel, wastel and cotchet. In all, she provided a rich and convincing account of life in the late 14th century. By contrast, when out of trance, Miss C. claimed to know nothing at all of this period.

These sessions greatly puzzled Lowes Dickinson of the Society for Psychical Research (SPR). He followed up all the statements of names, relationships and events; and, to his surprise, was able, in almost every case, to verify the truth of Blanche's assertions. This simply increased his puzzlement, for 'some of the facts given were not such as even a student of the period would naturally come across.' Blanche Poynings, for instance, was a relatively unimportant figure, merely referred to by two chroniclers as one of the Queen's attendants. So he concluded that the most likely explanation was

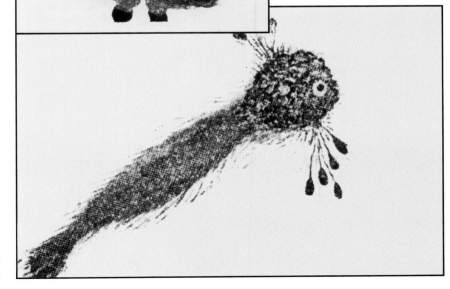

which is said to spell out messages without conscious direction on the part of those present when fingers are lightly placed on the board.)

Lowes Dickinson was amused by Miss C.'s claim that she could draw faces with the planchette and asked for a demonstration. The faces appeared but he found them uninteresting, so he went on to use the device for the more traditional questions and answers. At one point, he suggested that Blanche should be asked for, and the 14th-century lady immediately obliged.

A string of questions and answers brought out the unexpected name 'E. Holt'. This meant nothing at all to anyone present, but further answers spelled out by the planchette revealed that 'Mrs Holt... wrote a book... all the people are in it... I am there... *Countess Maud* by Emily Holt.' Once the name of the novel was out in the open, that was it: Miss C. remembered having read a book with that very title, and her aunt confirmed it. Yet neither of them could remember anything else about the book – not even the period it dealt with!

So a final hypnosis session was arranged, and Miss C. was asked to picture herself when young. When asked about her aunt reading *Countess Maud,* she was now able to describe the cover of the book and its main subjects. She went on to say: 'I used to turn over the pages. I didn't read it, because it was dull. Blanche Poynings was in the book; not much about her.' Then she confessed that Blanche now seemed to her to have no existence

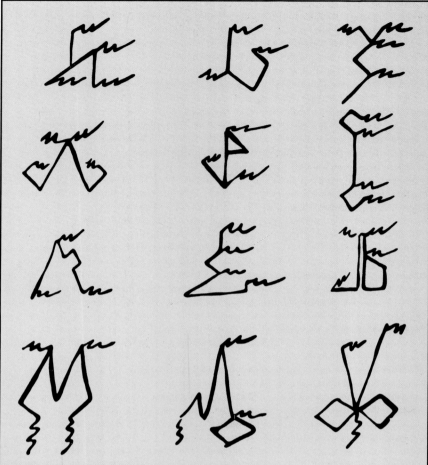

apart from the printed page: 'Nearly all the events [are] from the book, but not her character.'

Lowes Dickinson scrutinized the novel thoroughly and, with trifling exceptions, discovered in it every person and every fact referred to in the hypnotic sessions. But he also noted that Miss C. had exaggerated the importance of the minor character Blanche, and had ignored the order of events in the book and substituted her own plan. In this way, the whole of the borrowed material was skilfully presented in a natural way. He concluded:

'Her subconscious self showed in fact remarkable invention and dramatic power... so that if we had not happened to light upon the source of the information... it might have seemed a plausible view that Miss C. really did visit a real world and hold conversations with real people. As it is, the discovery... throws discredit on everything else, and especially on the elaborate details about her past lives with which Miss C.'s subconscious self favoured us.'

Much of the genealogical information that so impressed Lowes Dickinson occurs not in the main text of *Countess Maud* but in an extremely detailed appendix. Yet when Miss C. was asked under hypnosis whether she had ever read the appendix, she denied this and said that her aunt had never read her this part of the book. Yet it is clear from a comparison of the appendix with the accounts given by 'Blanche Poynings' that it cannot be the case. This confirms the necessity of treating testimony given under hypnosis with the greatest of caution.

In 1906, a clergyman's daughter, known as Miss C., claimed she had received communications from a woman calling herself Blanche Poynings. Allegedly, Blanche had lived during the reign of Richard II, right, and had been a friend of the Countess of Salisbury. She appeared to speak convincingly of the Countess' private life and of contemporary court events.

During seances, Hélène Smith wrote down the two pieces of Martian script, shown left and below left, and translated some of the symbols.

"" YET THE

MANY PEC

THE DEE

HAVE THE PROFOUND EXPERIENCE

OF ENCOUNTERING WITHIN

THEMSELVES A COMPLETELY NEW

INDIVIDUAL WHO SEEMS TO HAVE NO

CONNECTION AT ALL WITH THEIR

PRESENT EXISTENCE. ""

PETER MOSS AND JOE KEETON,

ENCOUNTERS WITH THE PAST

*In*FOCUS

THE SLEEP OF REASON

Cases of somnambulism, or sleep-walking, fascinated the Victorians. They believed that, when people sleepwalk, information that had long been lost in the subconscious tends to resurface. This interest has provided us with some fascinating case histories that lend weight to theories about obscure knowledge.

The frontispiece to the novel Sylvester Sound The Somnambulist by Henry Cockton, published in 1841, is shown right. The story drew on many well-attested cases of actual somnambulism.

One, recorded by Dr Dyce of Aberdeen, involved a servant girl who was subject to bouts of 'hypnotic sleep' during the day. In the course of one of these sleeps, she carried out her everyday duties without being in any way aware of what was going on around her. In another, she repeated the entire baptismal service of the Church of England – although she was unable to do so when awake. And, on one occasion, she sat through a church service in a trance-like state and was so moved by the sermon that she burst into tears – although she could not afterwards remember anything about it. However, in her next sleep, she gave an accurate account of that service.

But Dr Dyce's contemporary, a certain Dr Abercrombie, recorded a much more remarkable case involving the strange powers of a very dull and awkward servant girl who, once she went into a sleep-like trance, became gifted and erudite.

Dr Abercrombie noted that her language was always fluent and exact, and that her imagery was always appropriate and eloquent. Her most amazing feat, however, was giving a remarkable imitation of a violin playing. First, she made the sound of the instrument being tuned up, and then imitated a practice session, finally 'playing' a more elaborate piece.

It turned out that she had grown up in a farmhouse in which her sleeping quarters had one very thin wall. The bedroom on the other side belonged to an itinerant fiddler. Each night, he went through his repertoire while she slept. The music had obviously lodged in her subconscious, but it surfaced only during a trance-like sleep. Similarly, the ability to speak articulately and fluently was traced back to the conversations she had overheard in the schoolroom of the main house. This 'remarkable affection' lasted at least 10 years.

WHAT A COINCIDENCE!

EVERY ONE OF US HAS, AT SOME TIME, EXPERIENCED A COINCIDENCE. MATHEMATICIANS EXPLAIN THEM AWAY AS MERE CHANCE EVENTS – BUT THERE ARE THOSE WHO SEEK DEEPER REASONS

Shortly after British actor Anthony Hopkins had been chosen for a part in the film *The Girl from Petrovka,* he decided he ought to read the novel by George Feifer, from which the screenplay was taken. He could not find it in a single London bookshop, however. Then, while waiting for a train at Leicester Square underground station, he caught sight of a volume lying on a seat. Amazingly, it was that same novel. What is more, it

King Umberto I of Italy, above, was assassinated by the anarchist Bresci on 29 July 1900. Many important events in his life, as well as his death, were astonishingly closely paralleled by the life of another Umberto – a restaurant proprietor in a small town in northern Italy.

had scribbled notes in the margin. As Hopkins later found out, a friend had lost Feifer's own annotated copy, and it was this very one that Hopkins had come across.

Coincidences such as this certainly take one aback. Yet most of us actually have an intriguing coincidence of some sort or other to relate: bumping into a long-lost friend in some unexpected situation; suddenly thinking of someone who immediately telephones; humming a tune, and then hearing it on the radio seconds later; or even, perhaps, coming across an individual with your very own name whose life seems to run in parallel to your own.

One such occurrence involved King Umberto I of Italy who was dining with his aide in a restaurant in Monza, where he was due to attend an athletics meeting the next day. With astonishment, he suddenly noticed that the proprietor looked exactly like him. Speaking to him, he discovered that there were other similarities, too.

The most striking coincidences often involve the most commonplace of objects or occasions. One such bizarre incident was experienced by the Chicago newspaper columnist Irv Kupcinet, *left*:

'I had just checked into the Savoy Hotel in London. Opening a drawer in my room, I found, to my astonishment, that it contained some personal things belonging to a friend of mine, Harry Hannin, then with the Harlem Globetrotters basketball team.

'Two days later, I received a letter from Harry, posted in the Hotel Meurice, in Paris, which began "You'll never believe this." Apparently, Harry had opened a drawer in his room and found a tie which had my name on it. It was a room I had stayed in a few months earlier.'

The restaurateur was also called Umberto; like the King, he had been born in Turin – on the same day in fact; and he had married a girl called Margherita on the day that the King had married *Queen* Margherita. He had also opened his restaurant on the day that Umberto I was crowned.

The King was intrigued, and invited his 'double' to attend the athletics meeting with him. But the next day, the King's aide informed him that the restaurateur had died that morning in a mysterious shooting. Even as the King expressed his regret, he himself was shot dead by an anarchist in the crowd.

Another strange coincidence connected with a death occurred on Sunday 6 August 1978, when the little alarm clock that Pope Paul VI had bought in 1923 – and that for 55 years had woken him at six every morning – rang suddenly and shrilly. But it was not six o'clock: the time was 9.40 p.m. For no explicable reason, the clock had started ringing as the Pope lay dying. Later, Father Romeo Panciroli, a Vatican spokesman, commented: 'It was most strange. The Pope was very fond of the clock. He bought it in Poland and always took it with him on his trips'.

Many such examples of coincidences seem to defy all logic, luck or reason. It is not surprising, therefore, that the 'theory of coincidence' has excited scientists, philosophers and mathematicians for more than 2,000 years. Running like a thread through all their theories and speculations is one theme. Do coincidences have a hidden message for us? But only in this century have any real answers been suggested, answers that strike at the very roots of established science and prompt the question as to whether there are powers in the Universe of which we are still only dimly aware.

HIDDEN AFFINITIES

Early cosmologists believed that the world was held together by a principle of wholeness. Hippocrates, known as the father of medicine, who lived at some time between 460 and 375 BC, believed the Universe was joined together by 'hidden affinities' and wrote: 'There is one common flow, one common breathing, all things are in sympathy'. According to this theory, coincidence could be explained by 'sympathetic' elements seeking each other out.

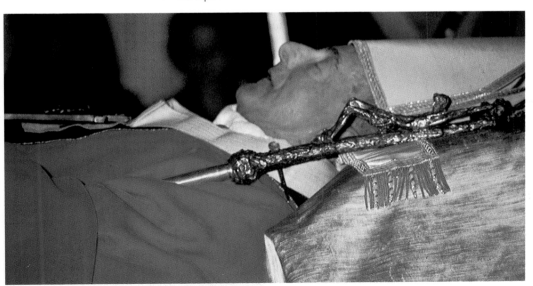

British actor, Anthony Hopkins, above left, was astonished to find a copy of George Feifer's novel The Girl from Petrovka *on a bench at a London underground station, having previously searched for one in vain.*

Pope Paul VI, seen left lying in state, experienced a strange event just prior to death. At 9.40 p.m. on 6 August 1978, his bedside alarm clock – set for six in the morning – inexplicably began to ring.

Similar beliefs have continued, in barely altered forms. The philosopher Arthur Schopenhauer (1788-1860), for instance, defined coincidence as 'the simultaneous occurrence of causally unconnected events'; and he went on to suggest that simultaneous events run in parallel lines.

These events, although links in totally different chains, nevertheless fall into place in both, he said, so that the fate of one individual invariably fits the fate of another.

PROBING THE FUTURE

The idea of a 'collective unconscious' – an underground storehouse of memories through which minds can communicate – has been debated by several thinkers. One of the more extreme theories to explain coincidence was put forward by the British mathematician Adrian Dobbs in the 1960s. Dobbs coined the word 'psitron' to describe an unknown force probing, like radar, a second time dimension that was probabilistic rather than deterministic. The psitron, he claimed, was capable of absorbing future probabilities and could then relay them back to the present, bypassing the normal human senses and somehow conveying the information directly to the brain.

But the first person actually to study the laws of coincidence scientifically was Dr Paul Kammerer, Director of the Institute of Experimental Biology in Vienna. From the age of 20, he had kept a 'logbook' of coincidences. Many were essentially trivial: names that kept cropping up in separate conversations, successive concert or cloakroom tickets with the same number, or a phrase in a book that kept recurring in real life. For hours, Kammerer also sat on park benches, recording people who wandered past, and noting their sex, age, dress, and whether they carried walking sticks or umbrellas. After mak-

ing the necessary allowances for factors like the rush-hour, weather and time of year, he found the results broke down into 'clusters of numbers' of a kind familiar to statisticians, gamblers, insurance companies and opinion pollsters.

SERIALITY

Kammerer called the phenomenon 'seriality', and in 1919 he published his conclusions in a book called *Das Gesetz der Serie (The Law of Seriality)*. Coincidences, he claimed, come in series – or 'a recurrence or clustering in time or space whereby the individual numbers in the sequence are not connected by the same active cause'. Coincidence, suggested Kammerer, is merely the tip of the iceberg in a larger cosmic principle that mankind, as yet, hardly recognises.

❙❙ CHANCE FURNISHES ME WITH WHAT I NEED. I AM LIKE A MAN WHO STUMBLES ALONG; MY FOOT STRIKES SOMETHING, I BEND OVER IT AND IT IS EXACTLY WHAT I WANT. ❙❙

JAMES JOYCE

Like gravity, it is a mystery; but unlike gravity, it acts selectively to bring together in space and time things that possess some affinity. 'We thus arrive,' he concluded, 'at the image of a world mosaic or cosmic kaleidoscope which, in spite of constant shufflings and rearrangements, also takes care of bringing like and like together.'

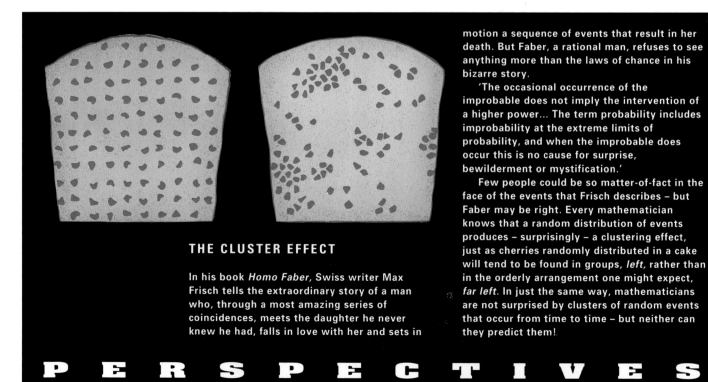

THE CLUSTER EFFECT

In his book *Homo Faber*, Swiss writer Max Frisch tells the extraordinary story of a man who, through a most amazing series of coincidences, meets the daughter he never knew he had, falls in love with her and sets in motion a sequence of events that result in her death. But Faber, a rational man, refuses to see anything more than the laws of chance in his bizarre story.

'The occasional occurrence of the improbable does not imply the intervention of a higher power... The term probability includes improbability at the extreme limits of probability, and when the improbable does occur this is no cause for surprise, bewilderment or mystification.'

Few people could be so matter-of-fact in the face of the events that Frisch describes – but Faber may be right. Every mathematician knows that a random distribution of events produces – surprisingly – a clustering effect, just as cherries randomly distributed in a cake will tend to be found in groups, *left*, rather than in the orderly arrangement one might expect, *far left*. In just the same way, mathematicians are not surprised by clusters of random events that occur from time to time – but neither can they predict them!

P E R S P E C T I V E S

*In*FOCUS

THE LIBRARY ANGEL

An extraordinary number of people report amazing coincidences when searching out information in libraries, so much so that Arthur Koestler coined the term 'library angel' to describe the mysterious force that somehow leads individuals straight to the right book.

Dame Rebecca West, for example, described how she was once confronted with whole shelves of works concerning the Nuremberg Trials at the Royal Institute of International Affairs, but the method of cataloguing was of no help at all to her particular piece of research. She even complained to one of the librarians, and demonstrated her problem by pulling out a volume at random. Not only was it the actual volume she needed, but she had opened it at precisely the right page for the data that she needed for her work.

Journalist Bernard Levin had a similar experience. He had been looking for a very long while for reference to a story about a statue of Alexander the Great. This statue was said to be so large that it could hold an entire city in its hand. He happened to be looking up another reference entirely in *Plutarch's Lives,* turned by mistake to the wrong page due to a misprint, and there found the story of the statue.

Sir Arthur Conan Doyle, creator of Sherlock Holmes, was also astonished to come across a story by de Maupassant, entitled *L'Auberge,* which was almost identical in every respect to a plot which he had been developing for a book of his own. It was even set in the very same inn at the Gemmi Pass in Switzerland.

More recently, astrologer and writer Derek Walters was assisted by the library angel when researching in the Chinese section of a university library. The information he sought was not readily available; what it more, his knowledge of Chinese was somewhat limited at the time, and there was no one to assist him. Suddenly, however, a volume fell from a shelf at his feet. Picking it up, he found it contained precisely the information required.

In his book *Coincidence, A Matter of Chance – or Synchronicity,* Brian Inglis, writer and researcher into the paranormal, also describes broadcaster Alistair Cooke's experience with the library angel. Pulling down a volume from a shelf, he noticed he had unfortunately picked the wrong one. In fact, it was on a different subject altogether: the *Good Food Guide* for 1972. However, he immediately realised that it would be just what he needed for a programme on the subject of inflation that he had to record in a few days' time, and he was able to find reference to a meal costing £3-4, thought to be rather expensive at the time.

Investigators are still puzzled by the nature of the phenomenon. Does the library angel really exist? Is it pure serendipity – happy chance? Or is some form of intuition perhaps at work?

The great leap forward happened when two of Europe's most brilliant minds collaborated to produce a most searching book on the powers of coincidence – one that was to provoke both controversy and attack from rival theorists working in this area.

These two men were Wolfgang Pauli – whose daringly conceived exclusion principle earned him the Nobel Prize for Physics – and the Swiss psychologist-philosopher, Carl Gustav Jung. Their treatise bore the unexciting title *Synchronicity, An Acausal Connecting Principle;* but it was described by one American reviewer as 'the paranormal equivalent of a nuclear explosion'.

ORDER OUT OF CHAOS

According to Pauli, coincidences are 'the visible traces of untraceable principles'. Coincidences, elaborated Jung, whether they come singly or in series, are manifestations of a barely understood universal principle that operates quite independently of the known laws of physics. Interpreters of the Pauli-Jung theory have even concluded that telepathy and precognition are also manifestations of a single mysterious force at work in the Universe that is trying to impose its own kind of discipline on the utter confusion of human life.

Arthur Koestler, above, wrote extensively about the search for a scientific explanation that would account for coincidences, or 'puns of destiny', as he called them.

But of all recent investigators, none wrote more extensively about the theory of coincidence than Arthur Koestler, who summed up the phenomenon in the vivid phrase 'puns of destiny'.

FICTION INTO FACT

One particularly striking 'pun' was related to Koestler by a 12-year-old English schoolboy named Nigel Parker:

'Many years ago, the American horror-story writer, Edgar Allan Poe, wrote a book called *The Narrative of Arthur Gordon Pym.* In it, Mr Pym was travelling in a ship that wrecked. The four survivors were in an open boat for many days before they decided to kill and eat the cabin boy, whose name was Richard Parker.

'Some years *later,* in the summer of 1884, my great-grandfather's cousin was cabin boy in the yawl *Mignonette* when she foundered, and the four survivors were in an open boat for many days. Eventually, the three senior members of the crew killed and ate the cabin boy. His name was Richard Parker'.

Such strange and seemingly meaningful incidents abound. Can there really be no more to them than mere coincidence?

Young girls of the Temiar Senoi tribe, **left,** *deck themselves with flowers before attending a trance ceremony during which the village shaman summons spirits to cure sickness. The shaman learns in his dreams of the special tune by which a particular good spirit can be summoned to overcome the bad influence responsible for someone's sickness.*

If the young Senoi boy, **below,** *prepared for the trance ceremony, wishes to become a shaman, he must have a dream in which he is 'adopted' by a spirit.*

WORKING WITH DREAMS

WE GENERALLY ATTACH LITTLE IMPORTANCE TO OUR DREAMS. BUT, AS THE SENOI – A MALAYAN TRIBE – HAVE LONG KNOWN, DREAMS MAY WELL BE CHANNELS FOR EXTRA-SENSORY-PERCEPTION

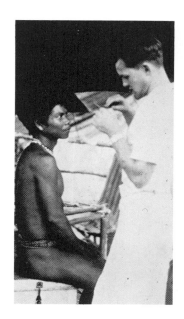

In 1932, British anthropologist, Pat Noone, was exploring a remote area of the highlands of the Malay Peninsula. During his travels, he made a first-hand study of a tribe called the Temiar Senoi. In Noone's view, they were extremely contented – he even called them 'the happy people' in his letters. Their marriages were lasting, and there was no history of crime or violence within the tribe. Their children seemed wonderfully content, too. Noone wondered what it was that made this tribe

British anthropologist Pat Noone, **above,** *devoted much of his career to investigating the dream life of the Temiar Senoi.*

so different from the superstitious, fearful, and often violent tribes that inhabited the surrounding area. To discover this, he spent the rest of his life studying the Temiar Senoi, and invited an American psychologist, Kilton Stewart, to share this work and contribute his professional expertise.

Noone discovered that the Senoi culture was largely based on the sharing of dreams. Every morning, the extended family would meet over the first meal of the day to tell each other their dreams and then discuss them. As soon as a child was able to speak, he was encouraged to tell his dreams. As a result, he would gradually become more familiar with his inner world and that of others, too.

All children have frightening dreams and nightmares, but the Senoi society is unique, as far as we know, in the way they teach their children to deal

with them. If a Senoi child dreams he is being chased by a large animal and wakes up in terror, his father might urge him to turn and face his pursuer in another dream. But if the animal is too large to be confronted by the child himself, he is encouraged to call on his brothers or friends to help him outface the animal in a dream The nightmares will then decrease and eventually stop altogether. The Senoi children also strike up relationships with the figures who have previously frightened them in their dreams, and in time these dream characters become helpful advisers.

The Senoi believe that the inhabitants of their dreams are the spirits of animals, plants, trees, mountains and rivers. Through their friendship with these spirits, Noone found, they believe they can learn things that they could never know by means of the senses.

One man, for example, who had befriended the spirit of the river in his dreams, frequently had dreams telling him where he could catch large fish. When he went to this part of the river the following day, he caught the fish he had dreamed about. On another occasion, he dreamed about the design of a new fish trap. He actually built a trap based on the dream design and found it worked very well indeed. Other men, whose spirit friends were of the animal kingdom, frequently dreamed of the best places to go hunting in the forest. Meanwhile, an aspiring shaman, or healer-priest, Noone found, would acquire a guardian spirit whom he would meet in a dream. He would go into a trance and lead the village in dances taught by the spirit, thereby winning recognition as a shaman.

Stewart also recorded evidence of much more obvious and powerful psychic phenomena in the Senoi's lives. On one occasion, when there was an epidemic in the tribe, a shaman had a dream in which his dead wife visited him. She taught him a dance, which she said would heal those in the tribe who were ill. In the dream, the shaman demanded evidence that she was indeed his wife and not some other spirit impersonating her. She said that if the dance were performed correctly, she would

Members of a dream group, led by Joe Friedman, are shown above. They would meet regularly to discuss their dreams, just as the Temiar Senoi do each morning. The members of the group found themselves remembering their dreams much more fully as a result; and, most remarkable of all, began to find telepathic and clairvoyant links.

cause a wooden box that was buried with her to appear in the middle of the long hut.

That night, the tribe performed the dream-taught dance: at the end of it, a box appeared in the air and fell to the ground. A cold breeze swept through the hut. Those who were ill quickly recovered.

Stewart and Noone were sceptical of this account, and so decided to hypnotise the shaman in order to discover the underlying truth. Under hypnosis, he recalled the story with only a few minor changes. It therefore seemed to them that he was not guilty of any conscious sleight of hand: indeed, he had been as surprised as anyone else when the box appeared.

Whether we believe this extraordinary story or not – and the value of the evidence offered under hypnosis is probably highly questionable – it is just one of many from cultures that believe dreams can have a direct healing effect. So can such phenomena also occur in our own society? Do we, too, have a psychic component to our dream lives?

In an attempt to discover more about the dynamics of dreams, in 1972, dream investigator Joe Friedman began to lead groups using the Senoi approach. Each week, a number of London adults aged between 20 and 50, often complete strangers, would meet for one evening to share and discuss their dreams. Each week, everyone would tell one dream that he or she had experienced in the days since the group's last meeting. The group would then try to clarify the events of the dream and the accompanying feelings.

THE SHARED DREAM

Although the main purpose of these meetings was to help members come to understand their dreams, it was found during the very first session that various kinds of psychic phenomena seemed to be facilitated. The most obvious among these was the 'shared dream'.

One group member, Bill, for example, described a dream in which he was standing within a semicircle with a magician, who reminded him of Tom, another member of the group. From the point where Bill stood, lines led to the letters of the alphabet. The magician told Bill that he was an 'H' or a 'K'. On the same night, Tom had a dream in which he was working at a post office, sorting parcels alphabetically into different bags. The correspondence here involved a person in Bill's dream who resembled Tom, assigning letters of the alphabet to Bill, while on the very same night Tom had dreamt of sorting parcels according to the letters of the alphabet.

Sometimes, one person's dream was even found to correspond with an event in which another member of the group had been involved the previous week. The following is a striking example.

Another group member, Peter, dreamed he was engaged in, or witnessing, a struggle between a scientist and the Devil. The Moon, which Peter could see out of the window, turned blood-red, became full, and came speeding through the window, rushing with great force towards the man's face. To quote from Peter's dream diary:

'The Moon had entered the man's head. I knew the Moon was one of the Devil's minions and here was the agent of possession... I saw the man

knocked against the wall... Then a small patch of red light shone on the wall next to his right hand.'

At that time, a fourth group member, Ron, having had difficulty getting to sleep, had been reading a fantasy book entitled *The Illearth War* by Stephen Donaldson. The part in which he was engrossed concerned a certain Thomas Covenant who was making a final attempt to overthrow the power of the King of Evil, Lord Foul. The power of Lord Foul was evinced by the fact that the Moon became blood-red and served as one of Lord Foul's minions.

In his dream, Peter saw a patch of red light on the wall next to the scientist's right hand. In the book, Covenant wears a white gold ring on his left hand. This ring emits a red glow during the period of Lord Foul's ascendance. Peter had never read the book, nor had he any ordinary means of being aware that Ron was reading it at the time.

Electrode-connecting wires festoon the head of a sleeping subject, above, in a sleep research unit. Infra-red video cameras in the unit's special bedrooms allow continuous yet discreet surveillance, so that periods of REM (rapid eye movement) sleep – during which dreams occur – can be monitored, while print-outs provide data on electrical activity of the heart, brain and muscles of the face and neck.

On certain occasions, the kind of extra-sensory perception that emerges in a dream is not linked to the present but to a future event in the life of the dreamer or another member of the group. Such precognitive dreams are often specific and accurate, and foreshadow events that are outside the control of the dreamer.

Yet we are normally unaware of dream ESP. Even when we do remember our dreams, they are rarely recalled in much detail for a long period, and we rarely make a record of them. Finally, even when we do remember and record our dreams, we rarely discuss them with others. If Bill had not been participating in a dream group, he would not have told the dream to Tom, since they were not close friends, and so he would not have discovered that Tom had experienced a similar dream the same night. There is, it seems, far more to dream content that is immediately apparent, as the Temiar Senoi have clearly long realised.

Recordings of a subject's brain waves, right, are made while she is awake, to be compared with her sleeping brain activity. Such records show that certain types of brain activity are much the same during dreaming as during waking life. But dreams do seem more conducive to ESP – perhaps because, when we are awake, our awareness of ESP activity is swamped by a profusion of ordinary experiences.

HOW DOES MEMORY WORK?

WHAT ARE MEMORIES? AND WHERE ARE THEY STORED? A STARTLING NEW THEORY PRESENTS US WITH MUCH FOOD FOR THOUGHT

We are all brought up to believe that recollections are stored inside the brain. It is an old and respectable idea, and many of us may not even think of questioning it. Nevertheless, the trace theory of memory may be open to doubt.

One of its earliest versions was put forward by the 4th-century Greek philosopher, Aristotle. He went so far as to compare memory with impressions that have been left on soft wax by experience – the sealing wax, the impressions left upon it, and the persistence of these impressions in the wax all providing an analogy with the process of memory.

One of the most widely accepted theories is that memories are laid down in the same way as music is stored in the grooves of a gramophone record, right. Much experimental work has been done in an attempt to locate these 'memory traces' in the brain, below; so far, however, they have been unsuccessful.

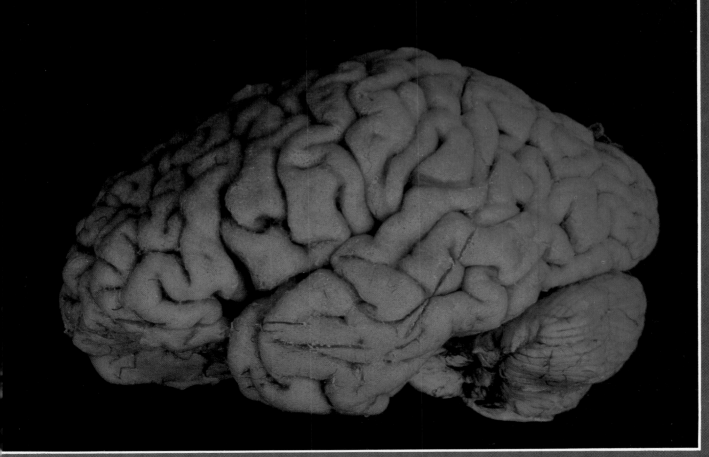

Since Aristotle, this same trace theory has been repeatedly modified in accordance with latest advances in technology to provide more and more up-to-date analogies. Currently most popular is the theory that memory is stored in the brain in the same way that information is contained in a hologram. This is a sophisticated version of the trace theory, but it is still essentially the same theory.

The trace theory applies to long-term memory specifically. But there is also another kind of memory, short-term memory. This is the kind of memory you have when you look up a number in the telephone directory. You remember the number for as long as it takes you to dial it, and then immediately forget it. It is possible that short-term memory is explicable in terms of a kind of reverberation in the brain's neural circuits. It is long-term memory that presents us with problems.

The hypothesis of formative causation suggests one possible answer. According to this theory, the development of form in living creatures is governed by a so-called 'morphogenetic' field – a kind of biological field that can, by a process known as morphic resonance, be 'tuned in to' by *other* members of the same species and so influence their development. This hypothesis can also explain memory to some degree. If organisms enter into morphic resonance with previous organisms of the same species on the basis of similarity, then there could be a very interesting consequence, for the thing that an organism resembles most closely in the past is itself. Although it is obvious that the development of individual living things is not governed simply by their own forms in the past, we nevertheless have the fascinating possibility that organisms may be subject to morphic resonance from their own past states.

Memory may thus consist of a kind of tuning in to the past states of our own organism through the process of morphic resonance so that the past is, as it were, continuously present to us. According to this theory, it is not necessary to suppose that all memory traces are stored inside the brain.

So why do we take the trace theory of memory for granted? There are two pieces of evidence that,

As a result of hydrocephalus – water on the brain – Sharon Scruton, right, developed a huge cavity at the centre of her brain; yet she had a successful school career. Using a technique known as PET scanning, it is now possible to identify areas of brain activity. The scans, below, show the brain in rest state, left, and exposed to language and music, right. A PET scan of Sharon Scruton's brain revealed that activities normally taking place at the centre of the brain now occurred at the peripheries – indicating that specific brain activities are not necessarily linked to particular areas of the brain.

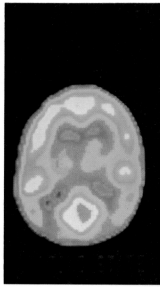

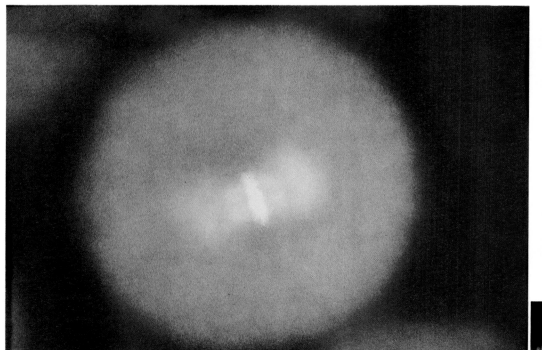

// WHEN YOU CONSIDER THE POSSIBILITY THAT THE BRAIN MAY NOT BE A MEMORY STORAGE DEVICE BUT, RATHER, A TUNING SYSTEM THAT ENABLES MEMORIES TO BE PICKED UP, THIS FAILURE TO FIND LOCALISED MEMORY TRACES IN THE BRAIN CERTAINLY MAKES SENSE. //

Early scientists, from Aristotle onwards, believed that memory was physically located in the brain. The illustration, below, from Margarita Philosophica by Gregor Reisch, published in Heidelberg in 1504, shows the seat of memory as situated just above the ear.

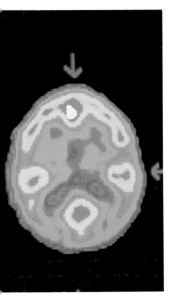

Cells are shown dividing in a sea-urchin's egg, above, far left. The development of such living creatures as the sea urchin, left, so the accepted theory goes, is governed by a complex chemical, deoxyribonucleic acid – DNA – that is present in every cell. But how does this explain the different ways in which different cells develop – into forms as varied as the sea-urchin's spikes and its luminous blue 'eyes'? A new hypothesis suggests that living creatures receive their form by 'tuning in' to a 'morphogenetic' field that contains information about the past members of their species.

might easily think so. And you might think you had proved you were right when you saw that, when you replaced the parts you had removed, the channel reappeared. Loss of memory through brain damage does not prove in any way that memory is stored inside the brain. It merely proves that a normal brain is essential for the effective recall of these memories. It is in fact possible that the effects of brain damage on memory can be explained in terms of the loss of the ability to recall or tune in to past states of the brain. Evidence from brain damage is therefore ambiguous.

A second piece of evidence often cited in favour of the trace theory of memory is related to the work of Wilder Penfield on electrical stimulation of the brain tissue of epileptics. He found that this enabled some patients to recall particular scenes from their past life with great vividness: indeed, the electrical stimulation seemed to reawaken memories. The most obvious interpretation of this result is that memories must be embedded in or near to the tissue that is stimulated, and that the electric current somehow reawakens them. But again, such supposed evidence is quite inconclusive. Think of the television analogy. If you were to apply electric currents to the tuning circuits inside a television set, you would find some very strange things happening – jumps from channel to channel, possibly, and distortions of the picture. But this does not prove that the figures you see on the television screen are actually located inside the television, any more than in the previous analogy.

CONFLICTING THEORIES

Further objections spring from the nature of the trace theory itself. Although the traces are taken for granted, their nature is still very much a matter of dispute in the scientific community. One popular and well-established theory suggests that memories may depend on reverberating circuits of electrical activity in the brain – loops of electrical current within the actual tissue. Another theory, which was much in vogue during the early 1970s, is the idea that memory is stored in the complex molecules of ribonucleic acid (RNA), a substance that is similar to DNA. The memory traces are, according to this theory, in some unspecified way laid down inside these molecules. However, this theory has rather gone out of fashion because there is very little evidence to support it, and it is not yet clear how a chemical or set of chemicals inside the brain can fulfil as complex a function as the encoding of memory.

But the third and most popular of theories is that of synaptic modification. The synapses are connections between the nerve cells, and the idea is that they somehow become modified as electric pulses – nerve signals – pass through them, making it more likely that the same signals will pass through them again. This is similar to the hydraulic theory of memory, as proposed by the philosopher and scientist René Descartes (1596-1650). Descartes suggested that memory depends on the flow of fluids through pores. The more often the fluid flows, the more it will enlarge the pores, making it easy for the fluid to flow in that direction again.

The main evidence for the theory of synaptic modification comes from a series of experiments

for many people, seem to provide conclusive and overwhelming evidence for the existence of memory traces, and that lead to the unquestioning acceptance of the idea that memories are stored inside the brain.

The more important of these is evidence from brain damage – that various types of brain damage can lead to loss of memory. A standard interpretation of this is that damage could remove those parts of the brain tissue that contain memory traces. But this is not the only possible interpretation. To see the fallacy in the argument, take the analogy of a television set. If you were to damage a television set by cutting out part of the wiring or removing a few transistors and condensers, and completely lost reception of one channel as a result, you would not automatically assume that this proved that all the people – actors, musicians and announcers – you saw on the programmes of that channel were contained within the condensers and transistors that you had removed. And yet, if you were embedded in that way of thinking, you

carried out on a species of snail, *Aplysia*. This snail has exceptionally large nerves, which are therefore easy to study, and it reacts in simple ways to simple stimuli: if you go on prodding it with a needle, for example, it gets used to this after a while and, instead of withdrawing into its shell, it simply ignores the prodding – if, that is, it has established that the stimulus is harmless. This is a well-known kind of learning, termed habituation, whereby animals simply ignore stimuli that do not threaten them.

Detailed and very elegant experimental work has shown that changes occur in the synapses of *Aplysia* during the process of habituation, but the reason for these changes is still unclear. There is evidence to show there certainly are, in some cases, changes in the brain during learning in the higher organisms – but can these changes explain the phenomenon of memory?

DAMNING EVIDENCE

The most damning piece of evidence against the trace theory of memory comes from a series of experiments carried out by K. S. Lashley. He set out with the hypothesis that, if memory traces do indeed exist in the brain, it should be possible to locate them. The idea was to cut out portions of the brain and identify the bits of memory that disappeared. He spent a great deal of time doing this and, after many years, ended up completely frustrated with this line of research.

Lashley's experiments were on rats, and he found that loss of memory occurred only when large portions of the brain were removed. Importantly, loss of memory was proportional to the *amount* of nervous tissue removed, rather than its location. Lashley called this the law of mass action: the idea was that it was the mass of tissue removed that was important, not the specific bits. The experiment was repeated with octopuses, and the same results were obtained: again, loss of memory was proportional to the mass removed, rather than the particular portion of the brain taken.

Clearly, all attempts to find localised traces within the brain have failed. This, of course, has posed great difficulties for the trace theory of memory, which had earlier seemed straightforward. It is, in fact, the main reason why the holographic theory of memory was developed – a modification that suggested that there are, indeed, memory traces, but spread all over the brain – so that if you cut out parts of it, you will not make much difference, since all memories are localised everywhere. But this theory, clear though it seems, is obscurantist. A hologram works on the principle of light waves and interference patterns stored on photographic film. There is nothing of the sort to be found in the brain.

This is the present state of research into memory. The idea that memory traces are stored inside the brain is really an aspect of the mechanistic theory of life, stemming from the theory that everything to do with the mind is explicable in terms of matter, and is reducible to things inside the brain. If you share this conviction, then you have to believe that memories are stored inside the brain.

However, when you consider the possibility that the brain may not be a memory storage device but, rather, a tuning system that enables memories to be picked up, this failure to find localised memory traces in the brain certainly makes sense. Several hitherto unexplained phenomena also begin to seem less surprising from a scientific point of view.

According to the new theory, we normally tune in to our own memories – but it is conceivable that the process of morphic resonance may allow us to tune in to other people's memories, too. Telepathy can thus be explained as the almost instantaneous transfer of very recent memories; and clairvoyance could be the result of tuning in to the memories of distant people. There is also, of course, the possibility of tuning in to memories from the distant past. This could be one way of explaining how some people can have access to memories of past lives, often through hypnotic regression. It could even explain why many of the memories produced under hypnotic regression are patchy, or seem to be the

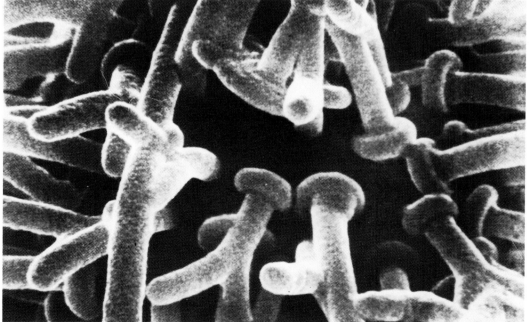

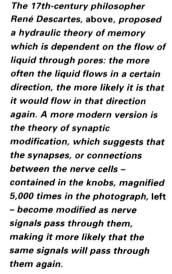

The 17th-century philosopher René Descartes, above, proposed a hydraulic theory of memory which is dependent on the flow of liquid through pores: the more often the liquid flows in a certain direction, the more likely it is that it would flow in that direction again. A more modern version is the theory of synaptic modification, which suggests that the synapses, or connections between the nerve cells – contained in the knobs, magnified 5,000 times in the photograph, left – become modified as nerve signals pass through them, making it more likely that the same signals will pass through them again.

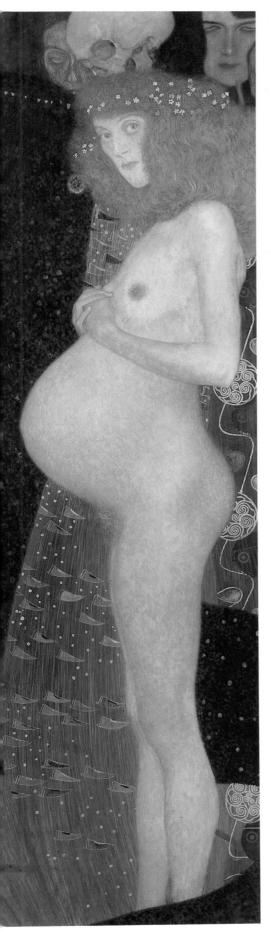

The main evidence for the theory of synaptic modification comes from study of the marine snail, Aplysia punctata, above, which shows changes in its synapses after undergoing a simple learning process.

In Hope 1, by Gustav Klimt (1862-1918), left, a pregnant woman stands surrounded by disturbing and phantasmagorical shapes. Could it be that, by means of so-called morphogenetic fields, our thoughts and actions influence human beings, as yet unborn, whom we shall never meet?

result of the overlapping of memories of entirely distinct lives. It could perhaps be the result of tuning in to more than one morphogenetic field at the same time, and jumbling the information received in this way.

This new concept of memory as an aspect of morphic resonance also lends theoretical support to the well-known notion of the collective unconscious, put forward by psychologist C.G. Jung. We may be influenced, perhaps, not only by memories of particular people in the past, but also by a sort of pooled or collective memory from countless previous human beings – in other words, there may exist a sort of species memory. Indeed, rather than existing separately, our minds may be influenced directly by others, including countless people in the past, through the interconnectedness of memory – whether we realise it or not. In turn, our own thoughts and memories may be adding to the collective memory of mankind, and may persist to influence future members of the human race, too.

" ... THERE IS NO REASON WHY CONSCIOUS MEMORIES – FOR EXAMPLE, MEMORIES OF PARTICULAR PAST EVENTS – NEED EITHER BE STORED MATERIALLY IN THE BRAIN OR DEPEND ON MORPHIC RESONANCE. THEY COULD WELL BE GIVEN DIRECTLY FROM PAST CONSCIOUS STATES, ACROSS TIME AND SPACE, SIMPLY ON THE BASIS OF SIMILARITY WITH PRESENT STATES. "

RUPERT SHELDRAKE,

A NEW SCIENCE OF LIFE

DOLPHIN INTELLIGENCE

SCIENTISTS AGREE THAT DOLPHINS ARE HIGHLY INTELLIGENT. CERTAIN RESEARCH EVEN SUGGESTS THAT THEY ARE BRIGHTER THAN HUMAN BEINGS IN SOME WAYS

Dolphins have figured in literature and art since ancient times. The fine dolphin fresco, far right, for example, is from the royal palace at Knossos, Crete, and dates from 1500 BC. The friendship of men and dolphins was often celebrated. On a coin, below right, from the Greek city of Tarentum, in southern Italy, the city's founder, Phalanthus, is shown riding on a dolphin. But a killer whale, right, closely related to the dolphin and nearly as intelligent, here shows itself less willing to be used as a mount.

A bottle-nosed dolphin – one of those lovable extroverts that delight the crowds at large aqua-zoos by playing with beach balls, leaping for fish, and even removing the top halves of bikinis worn by female attendants – learned to speak an English sentence with, admittedly, a strong Hungarian accent.

So said Dr John Lilly, a neurophysiologist who studied dolphins over many years.

The dolphin that allegedly spoke, and whose words were recorded on tape after being picked up on one of Dr Lilly's array of underwater microphones, made a simple enough demand. 'Throw me a ball,' it said, in a pronunciation suggesting it might have spent its calfhood in Budapest.

Not all those researching dolphin behaviour and intelligence are prepared to accept Dr Lilly's remarkable claim. He was trying, some say, to turn dolphins into 'floating Hobbits'. His theories concerning their intelligence were 'speculative to the point of irresponsibility', they say, stating that the vocal equipment of cetaceans – dolphins and whales – is quite incapable of ever producing human language. As for the English sentence recorded by Dr Lilly, it is clear, so it is asserted, that some electronic fault in a microphone caused it to pick up words spoken by Dr Kert, the Hungarian-born physicist who was leading a research team in the vicinity.

Dr Lilly remained unabashed. He was convinced that the words came either from Joe or Rosie, a dolphin pair that had frequently heard the voice of Dr Kert and that had picked up their English pronunciation from him.

Whatever the truth of the matter, there is no doubt that dolphins have a highly developed brain structure, more complex even than that of apes, and that they have a considerable native intelligence. They are also extraordinarily friendly to Mankind, noticeably lacking the responses of fear and hostility to human beings that characterise most wild animals.

This endearing friendliness was commented upon by Greek and Latin writers. The Greek historian Plutarch, for example, remarked in the first century AD that wild animals avoid men because they are afraid of them, that tame animals are friendly to men out of self-interest, because they are fed by them, and that: 'To only the dolphin, Nature has given that which the philosopher seeks, friendship for no advantage; though it has no need of any

man's help, yet it is a genial friend to all, and has helped Man.'

A century after Plutarch, the poet Oppian told a story illustrating the friendship between Man and dolphin. On the island of Poroselene, he said, lived a youth who, from childhood, had been loved by a dolphin. The boy would swim with the dolphin, play with it, and even ride on its back. The dolphin formed a strong emotional attachment to its human companion 'being fain to kiss and embrace the youth', and when the boy died, 'like one sorrowing, the dolphin visited the shores in quest of the companion of its youth: you would have said that you truly heard the voice of a mourner, such helpless grief was in it. And although the islanders called it often, it would no more listen to them nor accept food they offered it, and very soon it vanished from that sea and none saw it any more.'

For almost 2,000 years, this and many similar tales dating from classical times were taken to be no more than pleasant fantasies. Modern research and observation, however, have shown that there is

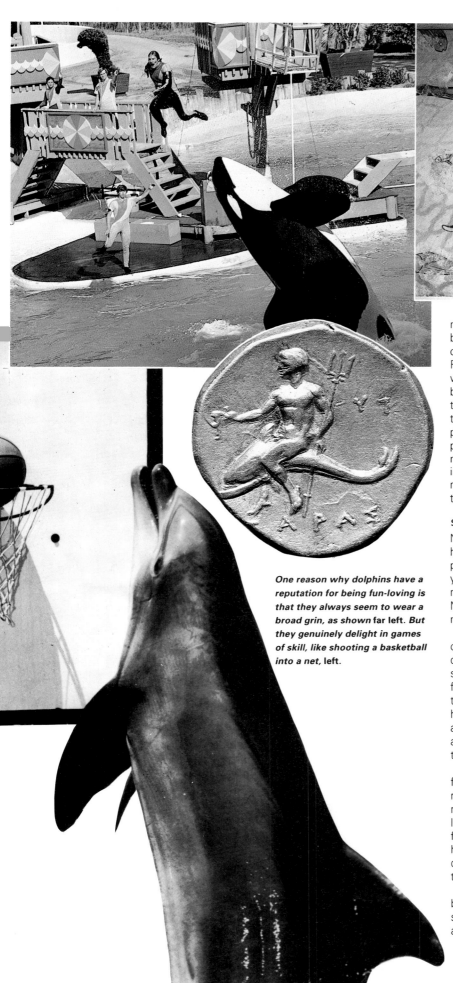

One reason why dolphins have a reputation for being fun-loving is that they always seem to wear a broad grin, as shown far left. But they genuinely delight in games of skill, like shooting a basketball into a net, left.

no reason to disbelieve the existence of a factual basis for such stories. Several present-day observers of dolphins, among them the writer Ronald Lockley, have experienced a relationship with dolphins similar in essence to that described by Oppian. Even the dolphin's supposed attempts to 'kiss and embrace the youth', which might be thought to be a flight of poetic fancy, are in complete conformity with modern observations of dolphin behaviour. Dolphins, like most advanced mammals, even seem to enjoy masturbating; and those in captivity have been seen to attempt to do so by rubbing themselves against humans swimming in their tanks.

SEEKING COMPANIONSHIP

Nevertheless, it would be wrong to think that human-dolphin friendship is only, or even usually, a product of the animal's sexual drive. Thus, Opo, a young female dolphin who, during 1955 and 1956, made friends with some of the inhabitants of the New Zealand village of Opononi, seems to have had no other motive than a desire for companionship .

Possibly she was an orphan – certainly, she first came to human attention when she began to nudge dinghies and other small boats in a manner that suggested she was looking for some lost parent or friend. By the autumn of 1955, she was allowing the crews of such craft to touch and even tickle her. Her liking for human beings steadily increased, and she soon began to swim into shallow waters and introduce herself to bathers, making it clear that she desired physical contact with them.

By the summer holiday – which in New Zealand falls at Christmas and New Year – a newspaper had reported her activities. Hundreds of sightseers made their way to the beach to watch bathers tickling and playing with Opo. She showed no signs of fear and even allowed some favoured swimmers to hold her. When introduced to a beach ball, she quickly learned to play with it, using her tail or head to throw it high in the air.

Opo did not like her human friends to be too boisterous in their play; if they became too rough she made no attempt to retaliate but simply swam away, indicating her displeasure by smacking the

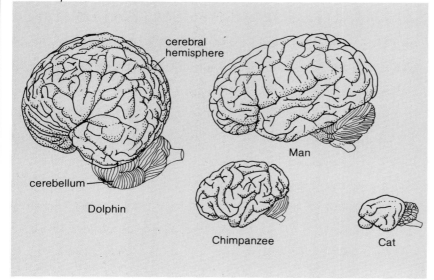

Brains of four mammals are seen drawn to scale, above. The dolphin's brain is slightly larger and heavier than Man's, but the human brain has a greater proportion of neocortex, responsible for higher intellectual functions.

The degree of development of the different parts of an animal's brain can often be related to a creature's way of life. The part of the brain called the cerebellum, for example, is responsible for balance and posture, and so is more highly developed in birds than in fish, for whom these functions are less important. In mammals' brains, the cerebellum has highly developed side lobes, which govern the movement of the limbs. In the primates, they regulate the delicate movements of the hands or paws, and of the fingers; but they are almost as important to the dolphin.

The distinctive abilities of the higher mammals are largely due to the neocortex, the outermost part of the cortex – the layer of nerve cells that covers the cerebellum and the cerebral hemispheres. The surface of the small brain of the cat is smooth, whereas the surfaces of the large brains of chimpanzees, men and whales are deeply folded. This folding results in a large surface area, and hence a high proportion of neocortex. Eighty per cent of the human brain is neocortex – more even than in the dolphin brain. Certain areas of the neocortex are concerned with specific senses; and the remaining 'association areas' are crucially important to intelligence, for they are concerned with learning. They form over three-quarters of the neocortex in the cleverer mammals – chimpanzees, humans and dolphins.

water with her tail. Children were her special delight, presumably because they were more gentle than adult swimmers, and she became a particular friend of Jill Baker, a 13-year-old whom she allowed to take brief rides on her back.

DEATH OF A DOLPHIN

One day, in April 1956, Opo was missing from her favourite playground. The next day, she was found dead, trapped by the shore in a rock inlet from which the tide had receded. It is possible that her liking for human companionship had killed her, that she had gone so near the shore in the hope of making new friends. One thing is certain: in the 10 months or so of her contact with human beings, she provided hard evidence that the classic 'fairy stories' of dolphins' friendliness and intelligence, and of dolphins with human riders, almost certainly had a factual basis. Even the tales told by ancient Greeks of sailors being saved from drowning by dolphins who held them above the waves until rescue arrived may well have been true. Certainly, modern observers have witnessed dolphin mothers spending many hours holding aloft sick calves, when their young have lacked the strength to reach the surface in order to breathe.

There are indications that the friendliness dolphins show to living beings of other species is related to their brain structure. The central nervous system of dolphins, like that of the other cetaceans, is very highly developed. It is difficult to compare the dolphin brain directly with that of land mammals, however. In the 30 million years or so since the mammalian ancestors of the cetaceans took to the sea, the dolphin nervous system has evolved in specialised ways that help it to survive in its marine environment. Much of this mechanism is not fully

understood. Nevertheless, the complexity of its brain is such that the dolphin is now generally regarded as more intelligent than other advanced mammals – the dog, seal or chimpanzee, for example. It is even possible that dolphins are more intelligent than human beings. The human brain has more neocortex, but the ratio of the dolphin's neocortex – its 'thinking brain' – to its limbic area – the oldest and most primitive part of the brain – is larger than in most human beings. This provides a clue to dolphin psychology. Evidence from human beings seems to indicate that damage to the neocortical 'association neurons' (nerve cells) correlates with impairment of the sense of humour, the capacity for emotional self-control, and the power of abstract thought – including philosophical speculation and problem-solving by insight. The high degree of development of the neocortex in dolphins suggests that corresponding faculties may be well-developed in these creatures.

So, while we cannot know whether dolphins engage in philosophic or religious speculation, there seems no reason to disbelieve that they are capable of doing so. It has even been suggested that they quite naturally go in the directions we call spiritual, and get into meditative states quite easily.

Whether dolphins actually meditate is likely to remain an unanswered question until someone develops a language that a dolphin can learn and use as a means of communicating with human beings. Such a step forward in the relationship between human beings and cetaceans is not impossible. At the University of Hawaii, for instance, Dr. Louis Herman, a psychologist who for some years worked with a pair of bottle-nosed dolphins, taught his subjects to understand a vocabulary of about 30 English words. The dolphins responded to these

words not only individually – which might indicate the type of learning by rote that is displayed by performing circus animals – but also in hundreds of combinations. Dr Herman also reported a curious fact concerning his dolphins' understanding of the word 'in'. This seemingly simple English word has several different uses: it can be a preposition, an adverb, an adjective – even a verb. When Dr Herman used it in a different way from any he had used before in his 'conversations' with dolphins, they showed an immediate understanding. This would seem to indicate that Dr Herman's pupils had acquired a rudimentary awareness of English grammar and wanted to use this knowledge in order to communicate with human beings.

DOLPHIN TONGUE

It has been suggested that dolphins have a language of their own – 'Delphinese' – in which they hold long conversations with each other. There is no doubt that they do communicate with one another. Experiments have even shown that, when two previously unacquainted dolphins are put in adjoining tanks, they use sounds as a means of communication. Clicks seem to be dolphins' usual mode of communication, but they also make a sound somewhat similar to human whistling. The behaviour of dolphins in this experimental situation always seems to follow a similar pattern: one listens politely while the other clicks away, then the talker falls silent in order to listen to the reply.

Various types of whistle seem to express distress of one sort or another – anything from a mild unease to the dolphin equivalent of a scream for help. Nearby dolphins, hearing a whistle of the 'scream' type, immediately hurry to the rescue and, even if their distressed fellow is not obviously in need of air, they push it to the surface in order that it may breathe easily. After the distressed creature has taken his first deep breath, there is often a prolonged exchange of clicks and whistles among the entire group. This was considered by Dr Lilly and others to be 'evidence of meaningful exchanges in the vocal sphere' – in other words, conversation.

It is difficult to devise experiments to test whether dolphins have the capacity for 'insight' – the ability to solve problems by thinking about them and then acting, rather than by blind trial and error. But observation of captive dolphins suggests that they do possess this quality.

Yet, in spite of the possibility that the communication barrier between Man and dolphin may be broken down, there seems little likelihood of our ever fully understanding cetacean consciousness. For dolphins have a sonic sense: they can 'illuminate' objects with sound pulses and, from the echoes, can judge the objects' positions. No human can understand what it is like to 'see' such a sound picture, any more than the sightless can understand what it is like to look at a sunset. We may one day come to comprehend dolphin intelligence, but may never share their perceptions of the world.

A trained dolphin 'stands' in the water, above, keeping itself up by thrashing its tail rapidly, as it takes food from its handler.

A US Navy trainer, left, holds out an acoustic homing device to a porpoise, Tuffy, being trained as a messenger for a Sealab underwater laboratory. Dolphins and porpoises have also been trained for more sinister purposes – as 'frogmen', to carry explosive charges and detonate them against the sides of enemy ships, for instance.

" IT HAS EVEN BEEN SUGGESTED THAT THE ACOUSTIC MEMORY OF WHALES IS SO ELABORATE THAT THEY COULD PERHAPS LISTEN TO AN ENTIRE SYMPHONY JUST ONCE AND THEN HAVE A MENTAL PLAYBACK LATER, REMEMBERING NOT ONLY EVERY PHRASE BUT ALSO THE WAY THEY FELT WHEN HEARING IT FOR THE FIRST TIME. **"**

LYALL WATSON, LIFETIDE

WHEN BIZARRE DREAMS COME TRUE

TALES OF CLOSE ENCOUNTERS OFTEN SEEM TO DESCRIBE SOME KIND OF PSYCHIC, RATHER THAN 'NUTS AND BOLTS', EXPERIENCE. WHAT PART MIGHT THE MIND PLAY IN UFO SIGHTINGS?

Many reports of encounters with UFOs and ghosts contain curiously similar or even identical elements. This suggests to the objective researcher that both kinds of experience may be psychic phenomena, originating in the mind. All such experiences are strongly subjective and often defy scientific explanation. Frequently, too, entities of one kind or another appear to a single person, while others who are also present notice nothing. Physical effects may be noticed by witnesses: tingling sensations and humming noises are linked with UFO sightings, while a marked drop in temperature frequently accompanies the appearance of ghosts. The vast majority of encounters with ghosts and UFOs occur at night, when the witness

Pendle Hill, below, is a traditional meeting place for witches, near Nelson in Lancashire, England. On 9 March 1977, Brian Grimshawe and a friend saw a dark, cigar-shaped UFO with flashing lights appear over the hill. It approached them, then drifted away.

The 'doughnut-shaped' UFO, seen in an artist's impression, right, pursued 15-year-old Frank Earp and two friends at Wollaton, near Nottingham, England. Then a huge, furry creature with 'legs that faded away into nothingness' appeared – but only two of the boys saw it.

It was at Cairo Mill, Oldham, England, below right, that John Byrne worked as a security guard. One night in 1972, he distinctly saw a huge, humming UFO hovering above him; but his colleague, who was nearby, saw nothing.

is alone or in some way 'vulnerable'. The two types of experience may seem to be very different; but, as the following examples also show, further similarities give cause for reflection.

In 1960, a well-to-do businessman of Manchester, England, was spending the night with a girl-friend when he suddenly felt the bedroom invaded by a curious tingling sensation. Soon, the air was full of an electromagnetic humming. Worried, he glanced around the room, and noted the time – it was just after 3 a.m. Then a figure appeared, standing by the bedside and blocking out the light that filtered through the window. It was a woman, only inches away from him and as plain and solid as the mattress on which he lay. His mind absorbed her features and her dress. Then he cried out. Quickly, the image melted into the blackness of night and he sheepishly awoke his sleeping companion to tell her of the ordeal. She knew what he had seen, for it was not the first time such a phantasm had appeared. The description matched perfectly that of the girl's dead mother.

Now to a supposed UFO sighting. It was not long after 3 a.m. on 9 March 1977, and Brian Grimshawe and a fellow night-shift worker were driving to their factory through the almost deserted streets of Nelson in Lancashire, England. Suddenly, a light appeared over Pendle Hill, famous for its long association with witchcraft. A dark cigar shape, flashing different colours, floated through the sky. As it approached, both the engine and the lights of the car cut out. The men became frightened.

They felt a strange tingling sensation, and an electromagnetic hum filled their ears. They tried desperately to escape the hovering UFO, but the car was dead. Then, just as suddenly as it had come, the UFO drifted away southwards. The car's lights and engine jerked back to life, and the oppressive sensations disappeared. The two men sped back to the factory, and soon developed pounding headaches as a result of their terrifying experience.

The materialization of a ghost and the sighting of a UFO... is that what these events actually were? That may well be. In any event, similarities between the occurrences are most intriguing and are duplicated time and again in other strange encounters.

INTELLIGENT CLOUD

Witness Frank Earp gives a graphic account of his own encounter at Wollaton, near Nottingham, England, in an issue of *Northern Earth Mysteries*. He was 15 at the time and playing with two friends beside a disused canal. He admits that they were looking for UFOs. As darkness came, a mist began to rise from the watercourse. This was not unusual. But then a cloud, the size of a fairground dodgem car, detached itself in the shape of a doughnut (without a central hole). It drifted towards them. Becoming disturbed, they quickly ran for home, as the apparently intelligent 'cloud' pursued them. They could all see it, glowing inside with a strange luminescence.

As they approached the edge of the village, they decided to stop. Frank was delegated to confront the 'cloud' for they were now close enough to home and could escape, should anything go wrong. Frank turned to find the cloud just 20 feet

> **"** OVER THE YEARS, I HAVE COME TO THE CONCLUSION THAT WHAT WE SEE IN THE UFO PHENOMENON THAT APPEARS TO BE PSYCHIC OR PSYCHOKINETIC IS, IN REALITY, SOMETHING WHICH... CIVILIZATIONS THAT HAVE FLOURISHED FOR PERHAPS HUNDREDS OF THOUSANDS OF YEARS HAVE MANAGED TO PERFECT. **"**
>
> **DR JAMES A. HARDER**

A common factor in stories about ghosts is the manner in which animals allegedly react, even before the presence is confirmed by a human observer. A family in Gorton, Greater Manchester, were plagued by a poltergeist in June 1981. The invisible force upturned settees, threw planks of wood around the living room and scrawled messages in toothpaste on household mirrors. Before these outbursts began, the family's Alsatian dog regularly became disturbed, running about, barking madly, and leaping into the air, as if trying to attack an unseen adversary.

A dog also plays a part in the following case, but this time there was no apparent ghost or poltergeist. Instead, there was a very peculiar figure, wearing a spacesuit.

The witness was an Army NCO, stationed at Dakelia barracks, Cyprus, in September 1968. At 3 a.m., his dog, a fierce Turkish wolfhound, suddenly sat up and began growling, its fur standing on end. Fearing a possible terrorist attack, the soldier went to the door, whereupon a high-pitched humming filled his skull. The dog was by now under the bed, whimpering and cowering. Out on the landing, the soldier saw, to his horror, the head and shoulders of a creature floating up the wooden stairs. It was humanoid and clad in a light blue suit. It had an eerie face that glowed orange, huge round eyes and a tussled shock of red hair. It could swivel its head through 180°.

The soldier rushed back to the sanctuary of his room, where he sat on the edge of his bed, shaking uncontrollably, as the whining outside rose to a crescendo. Now he could hear a sliding sound, as if the creature were approaching the door. He

(6 metres) away. He tried to ask if it was friend or foe, but his words were cut short by one of his friends, clearly terrified, tapping his shoulder and urging: 'When I say run – run!' He looked ahead into the gloom and quickly understood the reason for this fear. For there stood an extraordinary 6-foot (1.8-metre) furry figure, silhouetted in front of the glowing object. In claw-like hands, it gripped two red 'pencils', and its legs faded into nothingness. The third boy stood only inches from the creature. As the other two fled, he called after them, bemused. It later transpired that, although he was almost touching the figure, he had not seen it. But he *had* seen the cloud.

At Dakelia barracks, Cyprus, above, an NCO and his dog were reduced to nervous wrecks by the sudden appearance of a ghostly creature that floated up the stairs after them. Was it a real event, or perhaps some form of bizarre and terrifying nightmare, as in the photographic interpretation, below?

COMMON FACTORS

Experiences such as these pose a difficult question. Just where is the dividing line between different types of paranormal event? Does a dividing line even exist? Was the figure seen by that Manchester businessman really a ghost? Did the boys at Wollaton chance upon a boggart (a furry figure), a ghost or some other form of monster? There are no easy answers, but further examples of strange sightings may serve to cast more light on the problem.

At Cairo Mill, Oldham, England, on 8 October 1972, John Byrne, a security guard at the Ferranti engineering works, saw a massive UFO hovering above him. It emitted a strange blue light and a high-pitched humming whine; but his fellow guard, who was standing just yards away, saw and heard absolutely nothing – just as one of Frank Earp's friends had not seen the furry creature.

At Macynlleth, Wales, in July 1975, a terrified teenager saw a landed disc and undulating jelly-like entities which he assumed had come from it. The experience so shocked him that he suffered from persistent hysterical blindness for a long time afterwards. The disc became transparent in parts and blended into the surroundings before vanishing entirely – just like the traditional ghost which, it is claimed, one can see through.

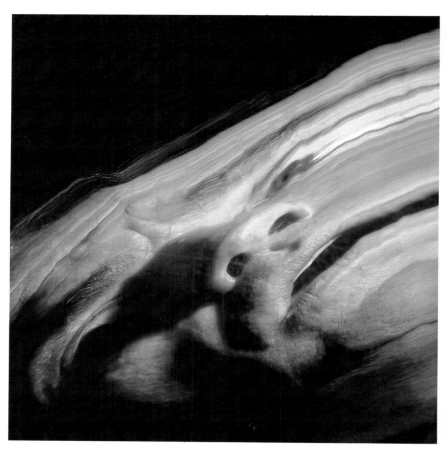

snatched up his underwater speargun, loaded it and aimed it at the door, whereupon the mysterious sliding noise faded away. An hour or so later, the soldier was found, still sitting on his bed and trembling with fear. And overnight, the dog turned into a quivering wreck.

A woman called Mary was driving her car near Norwalk, Connecticut, USA, in the summer of 1973 when the radio was suddenly filled with strange static interference. Suddenly, she heard a man's voice inside her head and found herself within a huge 'spacecraft'. How she got there, she has no idea. Standing before her was a tall entity with fair hair and dressed in a silver, one-piece suit. It conversed with her by telepathy, or directly from mind to mind. She was greeted with the strange words: 'Welcome my friend, Mary Angel.'

During the time the witness spent on board this 'craft', before being returned mysteriously to her car, the 'alien' gave her a tour of his UFO. It was supposedly peopled by no fewer than 200 crew, who came from what they called 'the galaxy of Guentatori-Elfi'.'The aliens prophesied specific floods that would occur in the USA. In due course, the prediction came true.

But aliens do not always display such insight. A woman in Belfast, Northern Ireland, was taken on board a UFO in 1976. She was told that Princess Anne would have twins and that Canada was about to join the European Common Market. Needless to say, several years later, these extremely unlikely events had still not come to pass.

One night in the early 1970s, two young men saw 'giant human brains' on a Californian road, above. Later, under hypnotic regression, one witness recalled humanoids with 'webbed features', as illustrated below.

Yet, perhaps it is a relief that these aliens can be remarkably human in their fallibility, for some of their prophecies are not so amusing.

Two men in their late twenties were returning from a night at a friend's house in Palos Verdes, southern California. As they were about to drive off, their headlights illuminated two weird shapes on the road. They were the size of basketballs and looked not unlike giant human brains. After observing them for a few seconds, they manoeuvred the car around them and hurried on their way. The driver then took his friend home (a five-minute journey), and continued on to his destination (another five minutes away), only to discover that two-and-a-half hours had gone by, not the expected 10 minutes.

The man, whom investigator Ann Druffel called John Hodges, was put under regressive hypnosis to try to restore his detailed memory of the event. He was anxious to find out what had happened to him. In this condition, he described how, when alone in his car, he was taken into a room and conversed telepathically with one of the brains. 'The voice comes within me... but it sounds like you are talking to me,' Hodges said. Some grey-skinned humanoid creatures with 'webbed' features were also present, apparently acting as crewmen. The giant brain showed Hodges 'advanced, three-dimensional holograms' depicting nuclear explosions, and explained that atomic power was being misused on Earth. Hodges later 'remembered' that the humanoids were, in fact, the real controllers and the brains simply acted as translation devices (alive, and yet not quite alive). A miniaturized 'translator cell' was implanted in Hodges' brain on the night of the contact, which would allow information to flow freely in the future. Eventually, he was returned to his car, but his memory was blocked and he felt a curious 'buzzing and tingling' all over his body.

Hodges received numerous subsequent messages via his 'translator'. These include information about a world war that was to erupt in the Middle East and then spread to Europe between 1982 and 1984. Nuclear weapons would be used it was said. After the war ended and a world government had been created, the aliens would land in 1987 and trigger the thousands of people who, like Hodges, had been implanted with 'translators' without their conscious knowledge. Time has proved otherwise.

Such a story sounds utter nonsense, and so do most of the other alien contact incidents that are reported. At the very least, however, they demand a reasonable hearing.

There is a considerable problem in trying to trace a common source of these incredible events for they are presented in many different contexts. They involve ghost-like beings, weird monsters, spirit entities, and a veritable menagerie of aliens from all over the Universe. Yet all of them share an underlying theme and many consistent internal characteristics. Are intelligent extra-terrestrial beings contacting us and behaving like skilled impressionists? Or could these experiences stem from a source that is somewhat closer to home – namely ourselves?

Consider this statement by John Hodges. 'The words... actually come from within the mind... loud, clear, crisp. The voice sounded male, but it's odd. It sounded as if it was the same voice I have to myself, when I *think*.'

witnesses – and only the scarf would be left lying on the ground. 'At last she has forgotten it', a sitter remarked. But, then, the scarf, too, would slowly vanish in the same manner.

Madame d'Esperance was one of the earliest English materialisation mediums and she readily co-operated with investigators who wanted to prove that her manifestations were not produced by fraud – even to the extent of allowing photographs to be taken. But one particular seance experience suggests that materialisation is not in fact entirely straightforward.

SMASH AND GRAB

At a meeting in Newcastle in 1880, one of the sitters became suspicious because another of Madame d'Esperance's materialisations – known as 'the French lady' – looked uncannily like the medium herself. He made a grab for the spirit, which promptly vanished. But the medium suffered a lung haemorrhage and was ill for quite a long time afterwards. On two other occasions, similar incidents occurred; but Madame d'Esperance was never officially found to be producing the strange manifestations fraudulently.

Spiritualists say that touching a materialisation (unless permission has been granted by the 'spirit') or putting a light on during a seance can do untold damage to the medium because it causes the 'ectoplasm' – from which the spirit forms are made – to return to the medium's body at too great a speed. Nevertheless, there have been a number of instances where materialisations have apparently been produced in daylight.

It was London medium William Eglinton who was responsible for convincing many sceptics. After

FLESHING OUT THE SPIRIT

CAN UNUSUALLY GIFTED MEDIUMS CAUSE THE DEAD TO MATERIALISE? SUCH CASES ARE NOT UNKNOWN, ACCORDING TO THOSE WHO PURPORT TO HAVE WITNESSED THE PHENOMENON

Yolande was a 15-year-old Arab girl. She was also allegedly a spirit, which meant she could appear and disappear at will in the presence of a famous English materialisation medium, Madame Elizabeth d'Esperance. The way in which Yolande materialised left witnesses in no doubt that she was a genuine paranormal manifestation, even though she appeared to be a normal living person in the course of each seance.

During one particular sitting, Yolande took a liking to a brilliantly coloured scarf that a sitter was wearing, and 'borrowed' it. When she dematerialised, the scarf disappeared with her. She was seen to be wearing it at her next seance appearance, and made it clear that she did not wish to part with the garment.

Sometimes Yolande's spirit form would gradually dissolve into a mist – on occasions, in front of 20

The photograph, above, was taken of the alleged manifestation of Yolande, the 15-year-old spirit-guide of the English medium Madame d'Esperance.

The illustration by Tissot, right, depicts the two materialised spirits he encountered at a seance given by London medium William Eglinton, top right, in the 1880s. It seems logical that a genuine materialised spirit would still be wearing a shroud; but, of course, voluminous clothing would also make an ideal disguise for fake 'spirits'.

attending one of Eglinton's seances, the famous conjurer Harry Kellar declared: 'I must own that I came away utterly unable to explain, by any natural means, the phenomena that I witnessed.' At one point during this seance, both Kellar and Eglinton were levitated.

One of the spirits who regularly appeared at Eglinton's seances was Abd-u-lah. He had only one arm and was adorned with jewels, rings, crosses and clusters of rubies that were apparently worth a fortune. Another materialisation, a bearded man in a long robe, allowed one of the sitters to cut a piece of material from his clothes and a part of his beard. These were later said to match holes in a piece of muslin and a false beard that were found in a truck belonging to Eglinton.

Despite this particular accusation of fraud – which was made by Archdeacon Thomas Colley – Eglinton continued to give seances and impressed many eminent people. He also developed slate-writing powers: spirits were said to write answers to questions on small black slates. The British Prime Minister William Gladstone visited him on 29

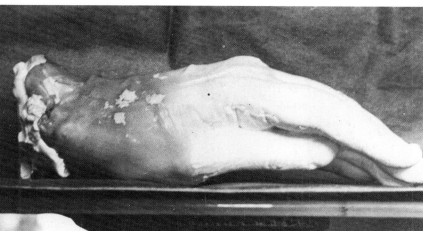

October 1884, and wrote down confidential questions in Spanish, Greek and French. The answers were given in these languages. Gladstone was so impressed that he subsequently became a member of the Society for Psychical Research.

The man who claimed to have exposed Eglinton was, ironically, no sceptic. Archdeacon Colley of Natal and Rector of Stockton, England, was in fact a staunch supporter of another materialisation medium, an English clergyman-turned-medium, the Reverend Francis Ward Monck. Monck was not only accused of being a fraud but was sentenced to three months' imprisonment on the evidence of 'props' found in his room after a seance in Huddersfield in November 1876. Archdeacon Colley was in South Africa at the time, but he was adamant that Monck was genuine.

The problem with materialisations is that they generally leave no tangible evidence. Investigator William Oxley, however, came up with an ingenious method of 'recording' the presence of Monck's materialised spirits – one that has also been used successfully with other mediums. At a seance in Manchester in 1876, Oxley began to make excellent paraffin moulds of the hands and feet of materialisations that appeared.

To make a paraffin mould, warm wax is poured on to the surface of a bowl of water and the materialisation is asked to plunge its hand into this. The spirit form then immerses its hand in a bowl of cold water, causing the wax to harden. The form next dematerialises, leaving a glove-like wax cast – often with a very narrow wrist opening, from which it would have been impossible for a human hand to withdraw without splitting the mould.

WAX IMPRESSIONS

A Polish intellectual, Franek Kluski, was a very powerful physical medium who also produced wax impressions. He was never a professional medium, but offered his services to Dr Gustave Geley and the Institut Métapsychique, Paris, in 1920. This eminent psychical researcher, and other investigators, testified that, in Kluski's presence, phantom limbs materialised, luminous forms glided around the seance room and brilliant lights suddenly appeared. Under strict controls, they were even able to produce photographs of a phantom. Both Dr Geley and Dr Charles Richet, who was a professor of physiology in Paris, obtained excellent moulds of materialised hands and limbs with Kluski. The full-form materialisations that appeared at his seances often arrived suddenly, though at other times they were seen to emerge from a faintly luminous cloud above the medium's head.

The materialisations produced by a Cardiff boot repairer, George Spriggs, seem almost too good to be true; but there is ample testimony from witnesses to the phenomenon who were all aware of precautions against fraud.

Spriggs' powers were first developed in a Welsh Spiritualist circle in the late 1870s. It all began with clairvoyance and automatic writing, and culminated in full-form phantoms. He emigrated to Australia in

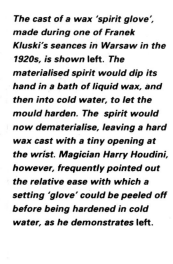

The cast of a wax 'spirit glove', made during one of Franek Kluski's seances in Warsaw in the 1920s, is shown left. The materialised spirit would dip its hand in a bath of liquid wax, and then into cold water, to let the mould harden. The spirit would now dematerialise, leaving a hard wax cast with a tiny opening at the wrist. Magician Harry Houdini, however, frequently pointed out the relative ease with which a setting 'glove' could be peeled off before being hardened in cold water, as he demonstrates left.

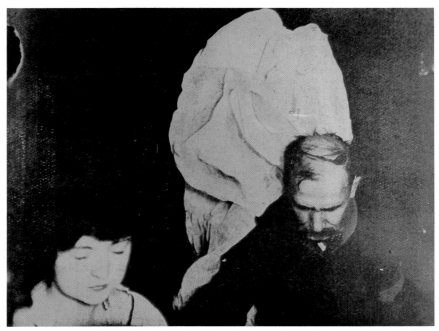

> I FEEL THAT THE AIR IS FILLED WITH SUBSTANCE, AND A KIND OF WHITE AND VAPOROUS MASS, QUASI LUMINOUS . . . IS FORMED IN FRONT OF THE ABDOMEN. AFTER THE MASS HAS BEEN TOSSED AND AGITATED IN EVERY WAY FOR SOME MINUTES, SOMETIMES EVEN FOR HALF-AN-HOUR, IT SUDDENLY STOPS, AND THEN OUT OF IT IS BORN A LIVING BEING CLOSE TO ME.

MADAME D'ESPERANCE

In the remarkable photograph, top, a phantom begins to materialise in the gloom of one of Kluski's seances. Spiritualists believe that ectoplasm – the substance from which materialisations are formed – is photosensitive. This is why most seances are held in the dark.

The Australian medium George Spriggs, above right, caused the materialisation of a spirit who wrote a letter and even went to buy a stamp for it, much to the consternation of the shopkeeper who sold it to him.

November 1880, taking his psychic powers with him. A prominent Australian named Donovan, a former member of the legislative Assembly of Victoria, attended Spriggs' seances for 18 months and wrote a book about his experiences.

PHANTOM LETTER

The Evidences of Spiritualism includes a report of an extraordinary incident that occurred at one of the Australian seances. A man materialised and said he wanted to write a letter to a Sydney woman who had visited the seances on a couple of occasions. He was given a pen and paper and wrote a three-page letter, which he placed in an envelope and addressed to the woman. But no one had a stamp. The spirit borrowed sixpence from a sitter and left the seance room to buy one from the shop next door. Word reached the shopkeeper that a phantom was on its way to buy a stamp. Utterly flustered, he forgot to give the dead man his change. The spirit realised the error when he got back to the seance and promptly returned to the shop for the money. The letter was posted and a reply received. This was kept until the spirit materialised at another seance, opened it, and read the contents aloud.

Spriggs' ability to produce materialisations faded after six years, but he developed the ability to diagnose illness psychically. He returned to Britain in 1900 and gave free medical advice in the rooms of the London Spiritualist Alliance.

Medicine also played an important role in the mediumship of English psychic Isa Northage, and the materialisation seances she gave are perhaps the most astonishing ever recorded. She was a popular medium in the 1940s, visiting churches to demonstrate her psychic powers, which included apport mediumship, direct voice and materialisation. But it was the healing work of her spirit guide, Dr Reynolds, that was in particular demand; and eventually a church was built specifically for this work in the grounds of Newstead Abbey, Northumberland. As Isa Northage's powers grew stronger, Dr Reynolds was able to materialise and carry out 'bloodless' surgery. This account, written by Group Captain G.S.M. Insall, is taken from a book about Isa Northage's mediumship, *A Path Prepared.*

'We prepared the room, donned white overalls and masks, as was the rule with Dr Reynolds. This

---

*In*FOCUS

THE APEMAN COMETH

Not all of Franek Kluski's materialisations would have been welcome at a party – if only because not all of them had a human form. In July 1919, an apeman made the first of several appearances at a Kluski seance. Dr Gustave Geley, present at many of these occasions, reported: 'This being, which we have termed *Pithecanthropus*, has shown itself several times at our seances. One of us. . . felt its large shaggy head press hard on his shoulder and against his cheek.

The head was covered with thick, coarse hair. A smell came from it like that of a deer or wet dog.'

Colonel Norbert Ocholowicz, who published a book about Kluski's extraordinary mediumship in Polish, in 1926, wrote: 'This ape was of such great strength that it could easily move a heavy bookcase filled with books through the room, carry a sofa over the heads of the sitters, or lift the heaviest persons with their chairs into the air to the height of a tall person. Though the ape's behaviour sometimes caused fear, and indicated a low level of intelligence, it was never malignant. Indeed, it often expressed goodwill, gentleness and readiness to obey...'

was not new to me as I had been a student in the most up-to-date French hospital before the first World War changed my career to flying... The two patients came in. [Both had hernias.] The first, the one with complications, was partially stripped and placed on the operating table.

'There was a trolley and I checked over the instruments – tweezers, swabs, kidney basins and bowls; no cutting instruments at all except scissors to cut lint. There was also a small white pencil light. I checked the emergency door and saw that it was locked and bolted on the inside, and draught excluded by a mat placed on the threshold. I was just closing the inner door leading into the church when somebody noticed that the medium had not arrived. I opened it again, and she came in. The light was turned low and somebody opened in prayer. I could see the medium sitting in her usual chair, a curtain hanging on either side.

'Immediately the prayer was over, a trumpet rose and Dr Reynolds' familiar voice greeted us all. He then reassured the patients... I was assigned a kidney basin to collect swabs and stepped forward to the operating table.

'The trumpet went down, and almost immediately the doctor appeared in materialised form on the opposite side of the operating table. He is of small stature. The medium was deep in trance .

'He first took the tweezers and swabbed the area with a disinfecting cleaner. The hernia was umbilical. I collected the swab in the kidney basin. Then I saw him place his hands on the patient's flesh, and they just went in deep, nearly out of sight. He stretched out for the tweezers and swabs and I collected eight soiled ones altogether.'

The materialised doctor checked that the patient was comfortable – he had felt no pain – and turned the pencil light on his flesh to inspect the area. There was no sign of a wound or a scar. Dr Reynolds then said he wanted to give the medium a rest before the next operation – and he dematerialised, vanishing in much the same way as others who are 'fleshed out' from the spirit world.

Charles Richet, top left, French scientist and psychical researcher, was president of the Society for Psychical Research in 1905. He was greatly impressed with the mediumship of Franek Kluski, finding no natural or fraudulent explanation for what he witnessed at his seances.

The three illustrations seen above, left and below, show three stages of materialisation based on the experiences of the medium William Eglinton. A 'mist' first emerged from the medium's side, and then began to form a shape, which grew to its full extent – here, in the shape of a hand.

Freda and Greta Chaplin, above, are twins who, since early childhood, have exhibited 'mirror-imaging' to an uncanny degree.

TWIN SOULS

SOME IDENTICAL TWINS BEHAVE SO SIMILARLY THAT THEY SEEM TO SHARE ONE IDENTITY, THE SAME PERSONALITY. IS THIS REALLY POSSIBLE?

Strange though it may seem, identical twins who are reared apart often exhibit more similarities of behaviour than those who grow up together. When they reach their early teens, however, most twins begin to develop a desire to assert individuality, even if this is expressed only by dressing differently. A few, however, fail to do this, and grow up as if they were one person.

One of the most striking examples of this phenomenon emerged in 1980 when the 38-year-old Chaplin twins, Greta and Freda, were brought before magistrates in York, England, charged with having behaved in a manner likely to cause a breach of the peace.

They had, it was asserted, been harassing Ken Iveson, once a neighbour of theirs, for 15 years, following him about, waiting for him outside the glassworks where he was employed as a lorry driver, shouting abuse at him, and even hitting him with their handbags. This extraordinary fixation, however, was not the reason that psychiatrists, social workers and journalists were so fascinated by the case: it was the fact that the twins spoke in what appeared to be precise synchronisation that intrigued everyone.

ACTING IN UNISON

Greta and Freda also exhibited other signs that seem to indicate that they were effectively one person – speaking, moving and dressing identically. Children in York even believed them to be witches, throwing stones at them in the street, while adults spat in their faces.

They once had identical grey coats, but as one originally came with green buttons and one with grey, they cut off two buttons each, so that both coats had two green and two grey. When given two different pairs of gloves, they simply took one from each pair. Similarly, a gift of two differently coloured bars of soap caused them real anguish. They burst into tears, then solved the problem by cutting the bars in half and sharing them. Once, when Greta got a prescription for bronchitis, Freda demanded the same medicine.

The twins have also be seen to eat in unison, slowly raising forks and spoons together, and both finishing up one item of food before starting on the next. But most uncannily, they appear to speak the same words at the same time, especially when excited or under stress. Careful listening, however, reveals that the words of one come out a split second later than those of the other.

They also exhibit 'mirror-imaging' which is characteristically found in twins that develop from a single split fertilized egg. In typical cases, one twin is right-handed, the other left-handed; the whorls of the hair grow clockwise in one and anti-clockwise in the other; and the left thumbprint of one almost matches the right thumbprint of the other.

The Chaplins also generally dress in mirror image of each other, although a casual observer would say they dress identically, and eccentrically, in their long skirts, clashing colours and headscarves. When Greta wears a bracelet on her left wrist, Freda might wear one on her right; and if one breaks a shoelace, the other has been known to pull out a lace from her opposite shoe.

Although the twins have been difficult and unpredictable to interview, some journalists have managed to talk to them. Some years ago, one writer elicited this telling statement from them: 'We're so close that we're really one person. We know exactly what each other is thinking because we're

The Chaplin twins first achieved national notoriety in 1980, when they were brought before York magistrates, charged with persistently hounding Ken Iveson, right, for 15 years. Their fixation with him became intolerable: they would lie in wait for him and shout abuse or hit him – this, it seemed, was their way of showing affection. It was their appearance in court that finally revealed the extent of their simultaneous behaviour. For many years, the twins, below, were the focus of many newspaper and magazine articles, and the centre of a medical controversy.

just one brain'. This journalist later remarked: 'You go gently for fear they'll disappear and leave you thinking you dreamed them up, like something from Alice in Wonderland'. She must have gained their confidence, however, because she did find out that they wear different underclothes.

The twins have also been seen to argue, sometimes hitting each other lightly with their identical handbags, then sitting sulking together for hours. But, if they believe they are the same person, then how can an argument happen?

A closer examination of their history shows that their extraordinary togetherness was actively fostered by their parents, especially their mother, who dressed them identically and allowed them no friends. They were not mentally abnormal and attended a secondary school near their York home. Teachers and fellow pupils remember them as neat, clean and quiet; and although among the slowest students, they could read and write as well as the others in their class. The deputy headmaster of the school had no doubts about what turned them into the disturbed adults they later became: 'It was clear that they had a doting mother who never allowed them any separate identity.... The other kids just

saw them as a bit quaint. I don't think they were acutely isolated then or maladjusted'. They had not, at that point, begun to speak simultaneously.

Their mother's attitude towards them seems to have triggered off a pattern of abnormal behaviour, perhaps aided by their biological affinity. Both parents seem to have been uncommunicative and friendless, and Mrs Chaplin was known to be obsessively houseproud. This emphasis on cleanliness may explain why at one time the twins' only apparent pleasure was bathing together, grooming each other, and washing each other's hair. They were said to use an average of 14 bars of soap and three large bottles of shampoo each week.

ACUTE HARRASSMENT

Ken Iveson – the subject of their harrassment – had grown up next door to the Chaplins, and married when the twins were two years old, continuing to live at his parents' home with his wife and children. Neither he nor his parents had ever set foot inside their neighbours' house; they were never asked in and never saw anyone else pay social calls. Iveson would, however, occasionally pass the time of day with the girls who, isolated from the outside world, obviously took this as some kind of romantic encouragement. They rapidly became a nuisance and, eventually, after 15 years, Iveson could take no more of it. Their case came to court.

The twins' parents had, it transpired, forced them to leave home. When asked about this, Freda and Greta reply as one: 'Something must have happened. Yes, yes, yes. Something strange. Must have happened'.

Mr and Mrs Chaplin refused to talk to the press, and exactly why the twins left is not known. They now live near London.

Curiously, local psychiatrists, called in by the court as expert witnesses, were baffled by the twins' case, describing it vaguely as 'a personality disorder'. Yet their behaviour towards Ken Iveson matches the textbook symptoms of *erotomania*, a form of schizophrenia in which there is delusion of being loved by a particular person. It has been recognised as a clinical condition since the mid-1960s. Dr Morgan Enoch, of the Maudsley Hospital

IDEOGLOSSIA, THE PHENOMENON IN WHICH TWO INDIVIDUALS, MOST OFTEN TWIN CHILDREN, DEVELOP A PRIVATE LANGUAGE, USUALLY INVOLVES HIGHLY ORIGINAL VOCABULARY AND SYNTAX.

in south London, has also discovered that if one identical twin is schizophrenic, then the other is also likely to suffer from the disease.

But does *erotomania* – or any form of schizophrenia – entirely explain the Chaplins' behaviour, especially their strange way of speaking? In their case, there seem to be many highly influential factors – genetic, environmental and social.

PRIVATE TONGUES

The Chaplins' peculiarity of speech is just one aspect of the way twins sometimes communicate with one another. Better known is *ideoglossia*, the phenomenon in which two individuals, most often twin children, develop between them a unique and private language. It usually involves highly original vocabulary and syntax.

It is, however, commonly confused with a subcategory, twin speech – a private collection of distorted words and idioms used, it is estimated, by 40 per cent of all twins because they feel isolated, or secretive, or both. Most twins tend to give it up at the age of three, although as twin Robert A. Nelson wrote to the *New York Times* in 1932: 'It is a matter of record in my family that when my brother and I first started to talk, and until we were well past six, we conversed with each other in a strange tongue of our own'. The only other person who could understand their particular speech was their brother, who was eight years older.

Identical twins, Grace and Virginia, were born in 1970 in Columbus, Georgia, USA, to Tom Kennedy and his German wife Christine. The day after the girls were born, Grace suddenly raised her head and stared at her father. Virginia did the same thing the next day. These strangely precocious acts, labelled 'convulsive seizures' by doctors, continued periodically for six months, in spite of treatment. At 17 months, they apparently developed *ideoglossia*, beginning to speak rapidly in a language of their own – their only concession to English being

'Snap aduk Cabenga, chase die-dipana': at this mysterious command from one of the Kennedy twins, left, they both began to play with the doll's house. Grace and Virginia were believed to be mentally retarded until it was discovered that they had developed a language of their own, complete with extensive vocabulary and syntax. 'Poto' and 'Cabenga', as they called themselves, were investigated by speech therapist Anne Koenecke at the Children's Hospital in San Diego, California. She finally coaxed them into speaking a little English and eventually discovered that their private language comprised both made-up and mispronounced words. It was clearly a vocabulary designed to exclude others.

'mommy' and 'daddy'. They called each other 'Poto' and 'Cabenga'.

When the twins were two years old, the family moved to California, but there were very few other children in the neighbourhood with whom Grace and Virginia could play. So they were left to themselves or entrusted to their maternal grandmother, Paula Kunert, a stern disciplinarian who still spoke only her native German.

In 1977, the speech therapists at the Children's Hospital in San Diego, California, began to study the twins, taping their conversation in the hope of learning something about the mysteries of developing language. Is it, they wondered, predominantly a product of genetic programming or a learned response to the world around them? A typical conversation between the girls would run:

'Genebene manita.'

'Nomemee.'

'Eebedeebeda. Dis din qui naba.'

'Neveda. Ca Baedabada.'

When the study began, the twins spoke no English, but gradually the therapists coaxed some out of them – which they spoke with a curious high-speed delivery. Someone even tried to talk to them in their own language, but they just looked at her as if she were crazy.

'Snap aduk, Cabenga, chase die-dipana,' said 'Poto' masterfully. Having apparently issued a command, she and 'Cabenga' instantly began to play with a doll's house.

Analysis of tapes showed that their communication was something less than true *ideoglossia*. Many apparently new words turned out to be mispronounced words and phrases from German and English, jammed together and said at high speed. However, a few words, such as 'nu-nukid' and 'pulana', remain unidentified. As the twins grew older, they suddenly began to speak English – but they remain silent about the meaning of their once private language.

CURSES HAVE ALWAYS BEEN FEARED –
WITH JUSTICE IT SEEMS, FOR
DISEASE, LOSS OF LOVED ONES
AND DEATH HAVE OFTEN
BEFALLEN VICTIMS OF SUCH
INVOCATIONS

A curse is an invocation of destruction or evil, part of the accustomed armoury of the priest, magician, shaman or ill-wisher. But do curses work and, if so, how? Swearing at someone gives vent to pent-up feelings; and most psychologists would say that ritual curses do nothing more – unless, that is, the victim is expecting trouble. Sandford Cohen, a psychologist at Boston University, USA, became convinced from field research that curses can be lethal, because of the feeling of utter helplessness they can inspire. Indeed, he sees a striking similarity between western Man dying from a fear of some disease generally believed to be fatal and primitive Man dying from a witch doctor's curse.

Another explanation involves the 'tape recording' theory – that a thought can imprint itself on an object or person, and also be transferred to others. If the thought is malevolent, so is the effect. There

The Mycenaean funeral mask, above, represents Agamemnon – according to Greek legend, one of the many sufferers from the ancient curse on the House of Atreus by Hermes. Agamemnon, the grandson of Atreus, was forced to sacrifice his daughter and was himself killed by his wife's lover.

NOTHING BUT TROUBLE

are, however, numerous cases of victims who were totally sceptical of supernatural 'mumbo-jumbo', but this did nothing to save them from the effects.

Take the case of Robert Heinl Junior, a retired colonel in the US Marine Corps. From 1958 to 1963, he served in Haiti as chief of the US naval mission, while his wife studied the voodoo religion. Afterwards, back in the United States, they wrote *Written in Blood*, a history of Haiti that was openly critical of the ruling dynasty of François 'Papa Doc' Duvalier. Then they learned from a newspaper published by Haitian exiles that a curse had been placed on the book, probably after Papa Doc's death in 1971, by his widow, Simone.

Initially, the Heinls were flattered that their book was thought to be worth cursing, but amusement soon turned to fear. First, the manuscript was lost on the way to the publishers, then it turned up four months later in a room that the publishers never used. Meanwhile, the Heinls prepared another copy of the manuscript and sent it off for binding and stitching, but the machine immediately broke down. Next, a *Washington Post* reporter who was preparing to interview the authors was struck down with acute appendicitis. The colonel then fell through a stage when he was delivering a speech, injuring his leg. And while walking near his home, he was suddenly – and severely – bitten by a dog.

Accidents continued, two involving the number 22, which Papa Doc considered magical. Finally, on 5 May 1979, the Heinls were on holiday on St Barthélémy Island, east of Haiti, when the colonel

Robert and Nancy Heinl, left, fell foul of the Haitian dictator, François 'Papa Doc' Duvalier and his wife Simone, below, while researching their book Written in Blood, *which was openly critical of Duvalier's regime. The Heinls believed that Simone Duvalier had cursed them, causing a chain of events that culminated in the sudden death of Robert Heinl. Nancy Heinl was in no doubt that a curse was responsible for their string of bad luck.*

than others.' Interestingly, the rabbi claims he failed to discover Shilo's mother's name.

In the Church of England, too, spiritual contracts are occasionally put out on church thieves. Since the 1970s, in Gloucestershire alone, two vicars have performed the commination (or divine threat) service – the Reverend Harold Cheales of Wych Rissington in 1973, and the Reverend Robert Nesham of Down Ampney in 1981. The commination service contains 12 curses and leaves room for more. It first appeared in the 1662 *Book of Common Prayer;* but in the 1928 revision, the word 'curse' was replaced by 'God's anger and judgement'. It was traditionally used against enemies of the Church on the first day of Lent, or whenever a church or churchyard had been desecrated. Christian curses seem to be, on occasions, just as effective as demonic ones: the old abbeys that Henry VIII seized from the monks after the dissolution of the monasteries in the early 16th century, for instance, often bedevilled their new owners over generations with the dreadful curses laid by angry monks.

A HEART OF STONE

There is a widespread ancient belief that no good will come from disturbing old stones or buried treasure: folklore worldwide is full of such tales, and the theme continues in the enduring popularity of the idea of a mummy's curse. Some researchers even believe that such deep-seated and widespread beliefs, as part of the collective unconscious, can exert a material influence, bringing myths to life and also reinforcing them.

The old castle of Syrie in Aberdeenshire, Scotland, is one such building plagued by a legendary curse. A group of stones in the local river is known as the Weeping Stones, one of which is missing. It is said that no heir to Syrie will ever succeed until that stone is found.

In 1944, when a 2-tonne 'Witch's Stone' was shifted from a crossroads at Scrapfaggot Green, Great Leighs, Essex, England, in order to widen the

dropped dead from a heart attack. His widow mused: 'There is a belief that the closer you get to Haiti, the more powerful the magic becomes'.

ROD OF LIGHT

Curses, precisely laid down in many rituals, are still cast by priests in many of the world's major religions. In September 1981, for example, Rabbi Moshe Hirsch, leader of the Neturei Karta, an orthodox Jewish sect, threatened to invoke the 'Rod of Light' against the Israeli archaeologist Yigal Shilo if he persisted in excavating the biblical city of David. This, the rabbi maintained, involved desecrating a medieval Jewish burial ground. Archaeologists, meanwhile, denied the very existence of such a cemetery.

The Rod of Light ceremony involves the reading of a text based on Kabbalistic writings. The participants burn black candles, sound a ram's horn and invoke the name of the cursed man's mother. 'This ceremony is an absolute last resort', said the rabbi. 'It has only been invoked twice in the last 30 years, both times with horrible consequences. There are many ways of dying, some that are less pleasant

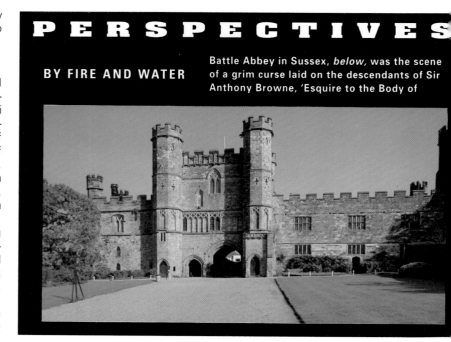

PERSPECTIVES

BY FIRE AND WATER

Battle Abbey in Sussex, *below,* was the scene of a grim curse laid on the descendants of Sir Anthony Browne, 'Esquire to the Body of

road, psychic havoc broke out. A great boulder was found outside the local pub, chickens were found locked up in rabbit hutches, rabbits ran loose in the garden, the church bells chimed irregularly, 30 sheep and two horses were found dead in a field, and a village builder's scaffolding poles tumbled about 'like matchsticks'. The 'Witch's Stone' was replaced and peace duly restored.

More recently, in 1980, a 30-tonne boulder was removed from the Devil's Marbles to a park in Tennant Creek, an isolated mining town in the Australian outback. Aborigines of the Warramungu tribe believe the Marbles are a relic from the so-called 'Dream Time' – when ancestral spirits created the world – and that any interference with such relics will lead to sickness and death. After the boulder's removal, a number of Aboriginal children fell ill with sores on their legs, and a tribal elder, Mick Taylor, warned that 'someone would get killed' if the stone was not returned. In March 1981, Mick Taylor died from meningitis at the age of 50. The town then agreed to return the boulder.

ROCKS OF WRATH

Curses that are inflicted as result of moving sacred stones are found in the New World, too. During the summer of 1977, airline vice-president Ralph Loffert, of Buffalo, New York state, USA, his wife and four children visited the Hawaiian volcano, Mauna Loa. While there, they collected some stones from the volcano despite a warning from the locals that this would anger the volcano goddess, Pele. Some claim to have seen Pele, who traditionally appears to warn of imminent eruptions. Shortly after they returned home, Mauna Loa erupted, and Pete certainly seems to have been angered, for within a few months, one of the Loffert boys, Todd, developed appendicitis, had knee surgery and broke his wrist; another son, Mark, sprained an ankle and broke his arm; his brother, Dan, caught an eye infection and had to wear glasses; and the daughter, Rebecca, lost two front teeth in a fall. In July 1978, the Lofferts sent the stones to a friend in

Henry VIII, Master of the House and Justice in Eyre', in 1538. Sir Anthony was cursed at the feast held to celebrate his ownership of the abbey by a monk who was angry at the seizure of Church lands during the dissolution of the monasteries.

The curse was specific: the family would die 'by fire or water'. It seems, however, that the curse went awry. Sir Anthony's other property, Cowdray House – which he had inherited from his half-cousin, the Earl of Southampton – was burned down; but this was much later, in 1793, after the property had passed into the hands of another family.

Antony Hippisley Coxe, compiler of the book *Haunted Britain*, records that the curse came into force yet again, in 1907, when the Duchess of Cleveland – renting Battle Abbey briefly – drowned in its grounds on her way to church.

A 788-year-old curse was ritually lifted by the former Chief Rabbi at the consecration of Clifford's Tower in York, above, on 31 October 1978. On the night of 16 March 1190, 150 Jews fled to the tower where they died by their own hand rather than fall into a mob's hands. The last to die was the rabbi whose final act was to curse the city of York. Until well into the 20th century, York was avoided by Jews, even though nearby Leeds has always had a thriving Jewish community.

'The curse has come upon me,' cried the Lady of Shallott, Tennyson's doomed heroine who is seen, right, preparing to meet her fate.

Hawaii who was asked to return them to the volcano. But the disasters continued: Mark then hurt his knee, Rebecca broke three more teeth, Dan fractured a hand bone, while Todd dislocated an elbow and fractured his wrist again. Mark then confessed that he still had three stones. They were returned – and the trouble ceased.

HEAD-ON CRASH

Allison Raymond of Ontario, Canada, and her family also took some stones away from the volcano. She told reporters: 'My husband was killed in a head-on car crash and my mother died of cancer. My younger son was rushed to hospital with a pancreas condition that's slowly getting worse. Then he broke his leg. My daughter's marriage nearly broke up and it was only when I posted the rocks back that our luck improved'.

Despite warnings, Nixon Morris, a hard-wood dealer from El Paso, Texas, took home a Mauna Loa stone in 1979. After returning, he fell off his roof, lightning struck an aerial, ruining several home appliances, and his wife fell ill.

Then Morris broke a hip and thigh when he fought with a burglar in their house. The family cat was sleeping under the bonnet of his wife's car when she started the engine: as a result, the cat was stripped of its fur down one side. Then Morris'

The Devil's Marbles in northern Australia, above, is a sacred Aboriginal site. In 1980, after one of the boulders was removed, Mick Taylor – a tribal elder – warned that this would lead to sickness and death. Several children fell ill, and Taylor himself died the next year at the age of 50.

At the Mauna Loa volcano of Hawaii, below, the Loffert family, on holiday in 1977, picked up some stones from the volcano – despite a warning that this would anger the local deity, the goddess Pele. Just as had been predicted, a series of disasters struck the family, ceasing only when the last stone had been sent back to Hawaii. Other tourists have reported similar runs of bad luck after taking away stones.

granddaughter had a bad fall and broke her arm in two places.

Morris also admitted that he had broken the rock in two and given a piece to a friend, adding: 'He brought the rock back to me after he wrecked four cars in less than two years'. Morris later sent the rocks back.

Jon Erickson, a naturalist at the Volcanoes National Park in Hawaii, at one time received up to 40 packages of rock a day from tourists who felt they should return them to avoid further disasters.

Skulls, too, frequently take revenge on those who move them. Lieutenant Commander 'Buster' Crabbe dived with the Royal Navy in 1950 in Tobermory Bay, Isle of Mull, in search of the Duque de Florencia, a payship of the Spanish Armada, which had been sunk in 1588 with a reputed 30 million pounds of gold on board. One of the trophies with which he surfaced was a skull that medical experts said had belonged to a North African

woman. Six years later, Crabbe disappeared, some maintain mysteriously, while on an underwater mission in Portsmouth harbour. The following year, a coroner decided that the headless body of a frogman washed up at Chichester, Sussex, was that of Crabbe himself.

The skull that had been found on the wreck was kept in the Western Isles Hotel, Tobermory, Scotland. One day, the barman accidentally caused it to fall and break. That same same day, he crashed his motor scooter and cracked his skull. He never returned to the island. The hotel owner, Donald Maclean, stored the skull away in a cupboard. In 1970, Richard Forrester, the new English owner of the hotel, drilled a hole in the skull so that he could hang it up in his cocktail bar.

'I was using an ordinary electric drill. The first odd thing that happened was that the metal bit of

*In*Focus

THE CURSE OF THE PHARAOHS –

Archaeologists can be said to be modern grave robbers – and, as such, often seem to have paid the price, for many ancient Egyptian tombs apparently carry curses for any who dare to desecrate them.

According to the American journalist Webb Garrison, Professor S. Resden opened an Egyptian tomb in the 1890s that was thus inscribed: 'Whosoever desecrates the tomb of Prince Sennar will be overtaken by the sands and destroyed'. Resden knew he was doomed,

it is said. He left Egypt by ship and died on board, a victim of suffocation with no discernible cause. Small amounts of sand were found clutched in his hands.

The poetic neatness of this story is, it must be said, rather suspicious and should perhaps be taken with a pinch of salt – or even sand.

But the 'curse of the pharaoh' continues. In September 1979, George LaBrash had a stroke while guarding the Tutankhamun mask, *left*, in San Francisco. In January 1982, he sued the city authorities for disability pay, claiming that the stroke was a job-related injury caused by the alleged curse on the tomb's desecration. The case was dismissed. The question remains as to whether this in itself was a refinement of the curse.

Film star Jayne Mansfield was killed in the appalling crash, above, on 29 June 1967. This was widely rumoured as being no accident. Jayne was said to have been cursed by her former friend, Anton LaVey, head of the Church of Satan.

Lance Sieveking, above right, broadcaster and father of author Paul Sieveking, demonstrated an unusual immunity to a curse laid by black magician Aleister Crowley by living 30 years longer than the curse allowed.

the drill, after piercing the bone, bent inside at an angle of 45 degrees. I found this surprising but thought nothing more about it. Two hours later, I was struck by excruciating pain in the back of the head. I was completely incapacitated for two days. Since then, I have been taking prescribed pills but the searing pain continues and never leaves.'

The only other person to handle the skull since the drilling had also experienced searing headaches.

RELATIVELY SPEAKING

The notion of a curse affecting a whole family is as old as civilisation. The ancient Greeks were firm believers in the efficacy of curses – the most celebrated affecting the house of Atreus. Atreus himself had killed the son of the god Hermes in a love contest, and as a result the deity put a curse on the murderer 'and all his house'. Atreus killed his own son by mistake; another son, the hero Agamemnon, was killed by his wife's lover; and she in turn was murdered by her son.

In Britain, several aristocratic families are believed to be afflicted by family curses. In the 18th century, the Scottish Earl of Breadalbane moved a graveyard to build the castle of Taymouth. According to tradition, a lady whose grave was disturbed laid a curse on the family whereby no two earls of this line would succeed each other. The prophecy apparently came true.

Even researching the subject of curses might be considered hazardous. In 1928, the occultist and magician Aleister Crowley ('The Beast'), met the young radio producer, Lance Sieveking, on the French Riviera. They spent many hours in conversation, and Crowley subsequently cast Sieveking's horoscope. It contained a number of predictions that were later fulfilled. One, however, was not. Crowley wrote: 'By the way, you will oblige me personally by dying at the age of forty-five'. Sieveking was then 32, but he disobligingly lived to be 75.

Crowley's curses, however, often claimed victims. The last was Dr William Brown Thompson, who withheld the addicted Beast's supply of morphia. In a rage, Crowley put a curse on him, saying that when he died he would take the doctor with him. Crowley died on 1 December 1947, aged 72. Thompson was dead within 24 hours.

" TWO HOURS LATER, I WAS STRUCK BY EXCRUCIATING PAIN IN THE BACK OF THE HEAD AND WAS COMPLETELY INCAPACITATED FOR TWO DAYS. SINCE THEN, I HAVE BEEN TAKING PRESRIBED PILLS, BUT THE SEARING PAIN NEVER LEAVES. **"**

RICHARD FORRESTER

TONGUES OF MEN, OR OF ANGELS?

Religious emotion overcomes one member of the congregation during a service at a 'Holy Roller' church, above. The other members are unembarrassed: their church regards such displays of emotion as perfectly natural. Pentecostalists often reach a crisis of religious fervour; and when the ecstasy is at its height, speaking in tongues may occur, as seen, left.

FEW EXPRESSIONS OF RELIGIOUS ECSTASY ARE AS DRAMATIC OR AS BEWILDERING AS 'SPEAKING IN TONGUES' – A BIZARRE, YET SURPRISINGLY COMMON PHENOMENON

The scene is set for an extraordinary – but by no means rare – phenomenon. A Pentecostalist minister's prayers grow more fervent; and the congregation's responses correspondingly increase in enthusiasm. Cries of 'Glory be to God!', 'Jesus, blessed Jesus!', and 'Hallelujah!' resound through the church. A woman rises from her seat. Her voice then swells until it drowns all the others, which sink into a chorus of soft murmurings. Now she begins to pour out a stream of completely unintelligible sounds – yet it is clearly passionate praise for the Lord. Minister and congregation then join in exalting the Holy Spirit of God who has granted their sister the gift of 'speaking in tongues'.

This phenomenon can be witnessed by anyone who visits a Pentecostalist church – although you may have to attend more than once as it does not automatically occur at every service.

Nowadays, 'speaking in tongues' implies *unidentified* tongues (or *glossolalia*). But before they could be recorded on tape, such sounds were often considered to belong to real, if unrecognised, human languages both ancient and modern (such as Incan and Eskimo), or even to be the 'tongues of angels'.

But since the advent of tape recorders and computers, not a single case of *xenolalia* (paranormal speaking in real languages) has been recorded; and the sounds that pour out so fervently at Pentecostalist services have been proved not to be languages but language-types. A linguistics expert can tell the difference by analysing the structure of the 'tongues' spoken. A personal knowledge of every language is not required; for the rule, to the expert, is quite simple – languages follow set laws

and language-types do not. 'Tongues' have neither vocabulary nor syntax, and so it must be concluded that they are neither the language of men nor, it has been assumed, of angels.

Although speaking in 'tongues' has been called 'refined gobbledygook', it is nevertheless a genuine form of worship. Indeed, it seems that this bizarre phenomenon enables people, who normally lack the ability to express themselves in public, to give vent to their religious emotions in such a way as to convince themselves and their fellow worshippers that the Holy Spirit is among them. It seems to uplift the congregation and give the speaker a sense of euphoric psychological release. But this form of communication, by its very nature, is emotional rather than educational – a sharing of mood rather than a conveying of information.

INTERPRETERS OF TONGUES

However, in almost every such congregation there is at least one 'interpreter of tongues' who sincerely believes that he or she is translating the 'tongues' into the vernacular. What is more, although the interpretation itself can help to reinforce the ecstatic mood of the congregation, it of course cannot be a translation or paraphrase of a language that does not exist.

Many Pentecostalists would deny that xenolalia has never been known in their churches, rightly pointing out that only a tiny percentage of all 'tongues' has ever been recorded or analysed. They also tell stories of numerous occasions when a foreign unbeliever, who is a casual visitor to the church, has been converted – by being preached at

The 11th-century Greek Orthodox mosaic, below, shows the Day of Pentecost. Jesus' disciples are said to have been baptised by tongues of fire, which released such an ecstasy that they shouted praise of God in many languages unknown to them. This was the first instance of Christian 'tongues'.

in his own language. Such a 'miracle' convinces the foreign sinner of the need to repent and join the Lord's church. Sometimes such a tale is told by the convert himself, sometimes by those who witnessed the alleged conversation. And since religious people are supposedly truthful, such reports are widely taken to be genuine.

RISEN FROM THE DEAD

Speaking in tongues among Christians first happened, so the New Testament tells us, when the disciples gathered in Jerusalem for the annual Jewish feast of Pentecost. This occasion was just seven weeks after Christ's crucifixion. The story is told by Luke (also author of one of the Gospels) in *Acts 2*.

 A WOMAN RISES FROM HER SEAT. HER VOICE THEN SWELLS UNTIL IT DROWNS ALL THE OTHERS... NOW SHE BEGINS TO POUR OUT A STREAM OF UNINTELLIGIBLE SOUNDS – YET IT IS CLEARLY A PASSIONATE PAEAN OF PRAISE FOR THE LORD. //

The disciples were worshipping at the Temple in Jerusalem, mingling with Jews from all over the known world, when suddenly they were seized by an ecstasy, said to have been caused by the conviction that Christ had risen from the dead. The 'Holy Ghost' is said to have descended on them, bestowing the 'gift of tongues' so that they shouted aloud their praise of God in all the various languages of the visiting worshippers, to the great astonishment of the crowd.

a sign of possession (except in the case of certain saints). Mainstream Protestantism has also found no place for it. However, it was kept alive down the centuries through fringe movements and heretical sects until, in the 20th century, it became the focal point for Pentecostalism.

SPREADING HYSTERIA

This movement started humbly, its members mainly drawn from ethnic minorities and poor people, and it was tainted at first – as its own historians admit – by hysterical behaviour and fanaticism. But it was a fast-growing movement, and quickly spread throughout the world, soon becoming by far the strongest Protestant group throughout predominantly Catholic South America, and surprisingly numerous even in countries such as Italy and Portugal, as well as in Protestant lands like Sweden.

Today, however, Pentecostal conduct and beliefs are more moderate; and in some of their churches, the emphasis on 'tongues' is not as great as it was originally. 'Tongues' now tend to be used more in private than in public worship. But possibly a much more important development in the use of

The 16th-century stained glass window, left, shows the conversion of St Paul on the road to Damascus. He warned against attaching too much significance to 'tongues of men and of angels'.

Objectively, however, the source of such xenolalia is not hard to pinpoint. Jewish religious law made attendance at certain festivals compulsory for every male adult Jew, but made allowances for great parts of the services to be spoken in the various vernaculars of the visitors present. So the disciples would often have heard what was recognisably praise of God in many languages, which they did not understand but which they probably stored deep down in their subconscious minds. Moreover, Christ had promised to send them his 'Comforter' – whoever or whatever that might be – specifically at the feast of Pentecost. This heightened sense of expectation, together with their conviction that Christ had risen, could have resulted in the first Christian 'tongues'. (The official account does not claim that the disciples understood what they were saying, nor does it mention that their utterances contained any specifically Christian message – it simply states that it happened, and astonished fellow worshippers.)

SACRED MANDATE?

The disciples' experience at Pentecost might have been considered unique in the annals of the Christian Church had it not been for St Paul's statement (in *1 Corinthians* 12-14) that 'tongues' were considered part of the normal worship of the Church at Corinth and that he himself was a glossolalist. Whether the Corinthian mode of worship was typical of that of the early church is debatable, but – despite Paul's warnings against abuses of 'the gifts of the Spirit' (especially the misuse of 'tongues') and his stress on the 'more excellent way' of Christian love – these references to Corinthian glossolalia have been taken by some sects as a sacred mandate to use 'tongues' as proof of 'baptism by the Holy Spirit'.

Since the early days of the Church, the use of 'tongues' has not always found favour among Christians, however. The Roman Catholics, for example, banned it from about the end of the first century, and later regarded speaking in 'tongues' as

A Christian convert, above, emerges from a baptism by total immersion, crying aloud with joy. Often the climax of such baptisms results in 'tongues' being spoken by one or more of the participants.

glossolalia than the spread of Pentecostalism is the Charismatic Movement, which has affected almost every Christian denomination today. Small groups in individual Anglican, Baptist, Methodist, Presbyterian and even Catholic churches now meet to worship God in private, using 'the gift of tongues'. Unlike the humble members of the original Pentecostal Church, the members of the Charismatic Movement tend to belong to the professional middle-classes, and they use 'tongues' in private, in quiet, unemotional prayer. Such people do not regard 'tongues' as being real foreign languages, but take them as a sign of the Holy Spirit's revitalising effect upon the Church, often enabling members to express the otherwise inexpressible.

The use of strange 'languages' is not exclusive to the Pentecostalists nor the Charismatic Movement, however. Since the foundation of modern Spiritualism about 130 years ago, hundreds of claims of spoken and written xenolalia by sensitives and psychics have been made.

HYPNOSIS IS A HIGHLY POPULAR FORM OF STAGE ENTERTAINMENT. NO ONE IS QUITE SURE HOW THE TRANCE-STATE COMES ABOUT; BUT THE TECHNIQUE CAN ALSO BE HELPFUL AS A FORM OF MEDICAL TREATMENT IN CRIME DETECTION AND IN EXPLORING POSSIBLE EVIDENCE FOR PAST LIVES

THE POWER OF SUGGESTION

Most people still think of hypnotists as slightly shady characters, practising a highly dubious craft. We see in our mind's eye the evil Svengali, the character in George du Maurier's novel who lived off the unfortunate Trilby, by putting the 'fluence on her so that she became an internationally acclaimed concert artist, though her ordinary voice was truly terrible. Today's stage hypnotist, however, is no longer the seedy villain of such a story – merely an entertainer.

Performances tend to follow a standard formula. Volunteers are called for; and one by one, the hypnotist addresses soothing words to them, like a mother putting her child to sleep. Those who respond remain on stage: the rest are sent back into the audience. Then, in groups or individually, those still on stage are told that they are very hot or very cold, very thirsty or very drunk; and they behave and feel just as they are told to do, even if they make themselves look ridiculous.

THE RIDDLE OF HYPNOSIS

There is not, as yet, any clear explanation of the nature of hypnotism. It is generally defined as a trance – that is, an altered state of consciousness, the extent of the alteration depending on the individual. In any group, some volunteers will remember everything that has been done while they are on stage, but others may recall nothing. Nevertheless, they all will have come under the hypnotist's influence.

What this means is that each of them has shed some of his or her controls, or thrown off certain inhibitions that training and habit normally impose. If somebody said to any of them, in ordinary conversation, 'You are a watchdog and you hear a burglar', it would raise only a laugh. On stage, however, the hypnotised subject gets down on hands and knees, and barks. The hypnotist is he-who-must-be-obeyed; and commands from other people are ignored, unless the hypnotist has given instructions that they should be obeyed, too.

Even more impressively, the accomplished hypnotist can give commands that will be obeyed after

subjects have come out of their trances and returned to their seats in the audience. If he gives them a 'post-hypnotic suggestion' that they should stand up and shout 'hip-hip-hooray' whenever the orchestra plays a certain tune, for instance, they will do so, without knowing why.

Hypnosis appears to switch off some part of our minds that ordinarily monitors our behaviour, instructing us what to do in any given set of circumstances without thought on our part. We hand this control system over to the hypnotist, much as an airline pilot may hand over the controls of his aircraft to somebody on the ground, who then guides it in by radar with the help of an automatic pilot.

Hypnosis has been exploited by tribal witch doctors and by priests in the temples of ancient Greece. But we owe the form in which it is practised today to Franz Mesmer and his disciples. Two hundred years ago, they realised that subjects in the trance state could be made to obey every command. But more importantly, in the course of their experiments, they made two discoveries of great potential significance.

Who, it is often asked, make the best hypnotic subjects? And can someone be hypnotised against his or her will? The hypnotist is, in fact, merely a guide; and his or her subject can only be 'put under' if the willingness is there. Often a trigger will be used – a snap of the fingers, perhaps, or simply a word or phrase – to induce the trance-state at a later stage. But, again, this will only work when the subject has every intention of cooperating.

Some stage hypnotists can give their profession a bad name. In one French hypnotist's show, *below*, a girl from the audience, apparently under hypnosis, stripped off. But it was the same girl every night! Hypnotist Martin Taylor, *below*, also gives stage performances. However, no compromising situations are introduced. In any event, it is highly unlikely that a volunteer would do anything outside his or her moral code. The hypnotised subject, *inset*, is merely obeying instructions to put on yet another tie.

For a start, they found that if they told a subject, 'You will feel no pain,' he could be struck, pricked and even burned without giving out so much as a yelp – and this was before the invention of anaesthetic drugs. Mesmerists further proceeded to demonstrate that pain-free surgical operations could be performed under hypnosis.

The medical profession refused to accept the evidence, however; and when distinguished surgeons were invited to watch the amputation of a leg under hypnosis, they insisted the man was only pretending to feel no pain. Hypnosis, they argued, was occult in its principles: it could not work.

The second discovery was that some hypnotised subjects suddenly found themselves enjoying talents they did not know they had in their ordinary lives. One might draw well under hypnosis; another, sing melodiously. A few even appeared to become

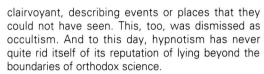

IF A HYPNOTISED SUBJECT IS TOLD HE IS GOING TO BE TOUCHED WITH A RED-HOT SKEWER, NOT ONLY WILL HE CRY OUT IN PAIN EVEN IF THE SKEWER IS STONE COLD, ITS TOUCH WILL OFTEN ACTUALLY RAISE A BLISTER.

clairvoyant, describing events or places that they could not have seen. This, too, was dismissed as occultism. And to this day, hypnotism has never quite rid itself of its reputation of lying beyond the boundaries of orthodox science.

Yet we know now that the Mesmerists' claims were largely justified. Endless demonstrations have shown that a subject under hypnosis can put his finger into a candle flame and, if told he will feel no pain, will feel no pain. Even more remarkable, if told he will have no blister, no blister appears.

Certain researchers have taken this even further. If a hypnotised subject is told he is going to be touched with a red-hot skewer, not only will he cry out in pain even if the skewer is stone cold, its touch will actually raise a blister.

Scepticism about the possibility that some subjects become clairvoyant under hypnosis has also been shaken by recent research into hypnotic regression. It has long been known that hypnotised subjects can be escorted back in time to earlier occasions in their lives. Asked to recall what they were doing on, say, New Year's Day 10 or 20 years ago, they will describe in detail episodes they have long since consciously forgotten. Where it has been possible to check such accounts, they have been found to be accurate. In the United States, the police have even exploited this faculty by asking witnesses of crimes and accidents to allow themselves to be hypnotised in order to find out whether they can recall, say, the number of a stolen car.

HYPNOTIC REGRESSION

Hypnotic regression has also been carried further. A hundred years ago, researchers in Europe found that some hypnotised subjects appeared ro be able to recall events from past centuries. Recently, this line of investigation has been taken up again, and the results are described in detail in works like Jeremy Iverson's *More Lives Than One*, an account of Arnall Bloxham's investigations, and Joe Keeton's *Encounters With The Past*.

It remains to be established whether such hypnotised subjects are regressing to their own past lives, or tuning into what might be described as a 'videotape from the collective unconscious', but it seems clear they are genuine. The material, even if not accurate in details, is certainly being picked up from sources other than books and conversations.

Hypnosis, then, involves a trance or altered state of consciousness, (some people prefer to describe it as a state of altered awareness of consciousness), in which certain faculties and abilities can be liberated. Clearly, the potential benefits, for anybody prepared

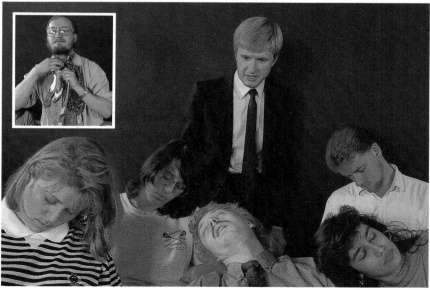

PERSPECTIVES

SELF-HYPNOSIS

Today, self-hypnosis is practised as a therapy by thousands of people worldwide. It has been used successfully as a technique for, among other things, reducing stress and tension, losing weight, giving up smoking, revitalising both mental and bodily energies, overcoming phobias and generally becoming more self-assertive.

One of the most popular forms involves the use of self-help cassettes. These usually start by relaxing the listener – often with soothing, light music or with sounds recorded from nature, such as the rustling of wind through leaves or the breaking of waves on the seashore.

Once relaxed, the subject is in a more fit state to take on-board suggestions and instructions that are long-lasting, if not permanent. Such instructions may be related either directly or subliminally.

to master the art of auto-hypnosis, can be considerable. Why, then, is more use not made of it?

Fear is partly responsible – the lingering suspicion that hypnosis is in the occult category and not scientifically resepctable, or the more reasonable fear that to undergo it is to put oneself into the hands of a Svengali.

WILLING SUBJECTS

Yet the fact that a stage hypnotists can so easily manipulate volunteers is somewhat misleading. The volunteers know it is a game. They choose to play it, presumably out of curiousity in most cases, and would not volunteer if they thought they might be made to do something dangerous, criminal, or even immoral, by their standards.

A celebrated occasion demonstrated this a century ago. A girl taking part in an experiment in Paris, who had been told to kill one of the students, appeared to try to do so and had to be restrained. Yet when asked to take off her clothes, she blushed, came out of the trance and ran from the room.

Presumably, she must have sensed in some way that she would be prevented from doing anything dangerous or criminal, and so agreed to join in. But actually to have undressed would almost certainly have compromised her own moral code to a marked degree – something unacceptable.

The implications of hypnosis for medicine are striking too; yet, until very recently, they have been largely ignored. It is only in the last 20 years or so that the results of research into hypnosis have been confirmed and amplified with the help of investigation involving biofeedback. These have shown how individuals can actually learn to control many bodily functions – heartbeat, blood pressure and gastric secretions, for instance – by auto-suggestion or self-hypnosis.

Hypnosis, or auto-suggestion, can also accomplish much more. Individuals, like the American Jack Schwartz, have even demonstrated how they are able to control bleeding, staunching blood flow as if turning off a tap. Similarly, it has been shown that much the simplest way to remove warts and other skin blemishes is by suggestion under hypnosis. It can also help in curing allergies and in getting a subject to stop smoking (though good hypnotherapists emphasize that they can only help those who want to help themselves).

PAIN CONTROL

The distinguished Australian psychiatrist, Ainslie Meares, and Americans Carl and Stephanie Simonton, have shown how hypnosis and auto-hypnosis can be used to help terminal cancer patients in particular, not merely by enabling them to control pain, but also by giving them a welcome distraction from their worries. In some cases, this has prolonged survival; and in others, X-rays have revealed actual regression of tumours. No false hopes of miracle cures are raised, as has so often happened with other forms of cancer treatment. Rather, patients are told that it is how they react to their own voyages of discovery in altered states of consciousness that counts.

Self-hypnosis has two major advantages. It can be taught, so that patients can learn to control, for instance, their own headaches and sometimes even prevent them. And it costs nothing – except, of course, for the practitioner's initial time in passing on the technique.

Post-hypnotic suggestion can also help in other spheres, such as golf. It will, for instance, send a golfer out onto the course in an utterly relaxed frame of mind – which, in golf, is said to be half the battle. Outside the medical field, too, it seems the possibilities for hypnosis are only just beginning to be appreciated.

IN TWO MINDS

SCIENCE HAS REVEALED THAT THE HUMAN BRAIN IS SPLIT INTO TWO – THAT, QUITE LITERALLY, WE ALL HAVE TWO INDEPENDENT BRAINS. WHAT ARE THE IMPLICATIONS OF THIS MOST EXTRAORDINARY DISCOVERY?

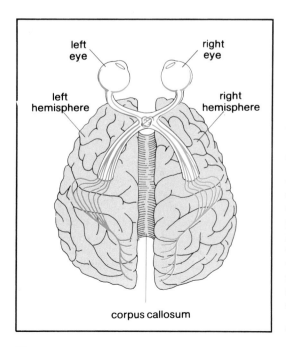

left eye

right eye

left hemisphere

right hemisphere

corpus callosum

One of the greatest achievements of the famous French mathematician Henri Poincaré (1854-1912) was the resolution of a difficult mathematical problem concerning what he called 'Fuchsian functions'. He says in his memoirs that he studied the problem diligently and logically for some time but failed to get a suitable answer. In the midst of intensive mathematical work on the problem, he took a short break to go on a geological excursion, where the excitement of the travel made him forget all about mathematics. So, with his mind full of geology rather than Fuchsian functions, he waited for the bus that was to take him on a field visit. The bus arrived – and suddenly, as he boarded it, the solution to his problem came to him in a kind of intuitive, unthinking flash. He was so confident that he had the right answer that he did not bother to verify his intuitive insight until he had returned from the excursion. His sudden insight, which turned out to be absolutely correct, had succeeded where logic previously had failed.

There are many instances in history of such 'flashes of insight' – many of them occurring in

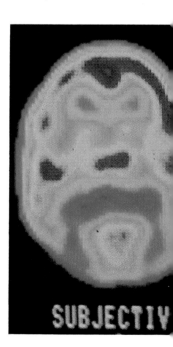

SUBJECTIV

RESTORING THE BALANCE

Mysterious powers that lie hidden in our right brain may prove to be the origin of a whole range of experiences that defy rational explanation. Among them are a number of psychic abilities.

Water diviners, for instance, often dowse in a relaxed, almost trance-like state in which the left brain does not assert its dominance and the right brain can act freely. It is possible that the right brain even recognises the presence of water and causes the arm muscles to contract involuntarily, making the dowsing rod move. The involvement of the right brain in psychic abilities may explain, too, why phenomena

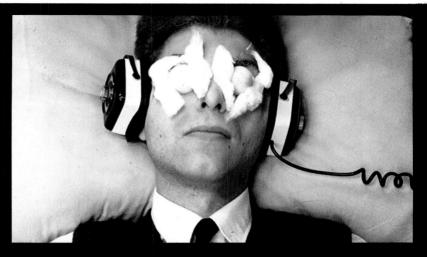

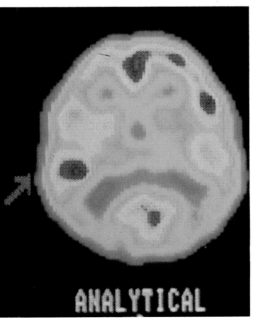

The abilities of the water diviner, left. and the subject of a Ganzfeld telepathy test, above, are thought to be controlled by the right brain.

like metal bending, telepathy and clairvoyance are so notoriously difficult to reproduce in the laboratory: the scientific environment of the laboratory may repress psychic abilities by actively accentuating the dominance of the left brain.

There is another startling possibility. Perhaps telepathy – apparently an elusive ability that surfaces only fitfully – is actually simply the way our right brains speak to each other. To restore the balance between left and right brains might therefore be to restore latent telepathic abilities.

PERSPECTIVES

The brain, as shown far left, is made up of two distinct halves, linked by a 'bridge' of around 200 million nerve fibres that is called the corpus callosum. The left hemisphere controls most of the right-hand side of the body, while the right hemisphere controls most of the left-hand side. The two hemispheres have different cognitive functions: broadly, analytical functions occur in the left brain while intuitive functions occur in the right brain. The brain scans, left, were taken while the subject was listening to music. In the scan on the left, he is reacting intuitively and subjectively – and the neural activity is predominantly in the right brain. In the scan on the right, he is listening more analytically – and the main neural activity is seen to have shifted to the left hemisphere.

dreams – that suddenly provide a person who is worrying over some problem or other with the correct solution. What is especially interesting is that these insights often occur when the person concerned is not consciously thinking about the problem. It is as if, by 'letting go' and allowing itself to wander away from strictly logical thinking, the brain can somehow provide the answers.

So does Poincaré's experience, and others like it, mean that the brain can work in two distinct ways – either in a systematic, step-by-step way, or intuitively, without conscious control?

The answer, according to a growing number of physiologists and psychologists, appears to be 'yes': that is, our brain does seem to operate both logically and intuitively, and will oscillate between these two distinct forms of behaviour according to circumstances.

Work carried out by anatomists and neurophysiologists, who study the brain and its functions, supports this claim. Anatomically, we know that the human body is roughly bilaterally symmetrical. It is possible to draw an imaginary line through the middle of a person, bisecting the nose and ending between the feet and, with a few rather important exceptions – such as the heart – the right side of the body is seen as a mirror image of the left side. On a general anatomical level, this also holds true for the brain.

Looked at from above, the brain is made up of two cerebral hemispheres. Joining these two hemispheres is a bridge that comprises about 200 million nerve fibres called the *corpus callosum*. This structure is one of several bundles of nerve fibres, linking equivalent centres on the two sides of the brain. Now, although each hemisphere of the brain appears to be the approximate mirror image of the other, this is not the case: when the hemispheres are examined more closely, profound differences emerge between the functions of the left and right sides.

There are, of course, other instances of seemingly symmetrical parts of the body that, although mirroring each other anatomically, are actually rather different functionally. The most obvious example is our hands: 90 per cent of people write using their right hand and are termed 'right-hand dominant'. In these people, the left hand is termed the 'minor' hand. The 10 per cent of people who write with their left hand are 'left-hand dominant'.

The two hemispheres of the brain also show this 'dominant-minor' distinction, but in this case, the left side of the brain is usually the dominant side (for 96 – 98 per cent of the population), the right hemisphere taking the 'minor' role.

It may seem curious at first that, although the left hemisphere of the brain is dominant, it is the right hand, in most people, that is dominant. But there is a straightforward anatomical explanation: in the hind-brain (the rearmost part of the brain, continuous with the upper end of the spinal cord), many bundles of nerve fibres 'decussate' (cross over) from right to left, and vice versa. This decussation of fibres is responsible for the fact that the left side of the brain generally controls the right side of the body, and vice versa. So it is that the dominant left hemisphere of the brain controls the dominant right hand.

ROOTS OF DEXTERITY

But what exactly does it mean to say that the left hemisphere of the brain is dominant? Dominance in a hand is quite clear. It is stronger and more dextrous. The brain, however, encased in its hard skull, is much more of an enigma. Perhaps not surprisingly, it was not until 1844 that it was proposed – by A. L. Wigan, in his book *The Duality of Mind* – that the fact that the brain has two hemispheres might mean that people have two separate minds. This extremely controversial idea was suggested to Wigan by a post-mortem examination he carried out on a man with no history of mental illness, whose brain turned out to have only one hemisphere. The fact that half his brain was missing had apparently produced no noticeable effect during his life.

This was the first recorded instance of extreme one-hemisphere dominance. Although more recent anatomical evidence has been less dramatic, neurophysiologists probing the brain have found many examples in which one hemisphere dominates the other in specific ranges of functions.

One important method of examining the functions of the two sides of the brain is 'split-brain' research. Splitting the brain means carrying out a commissurotomy – that is, cutting the *corpus callosum* which, as we have seen, is a thick bundle of nerve fibres connecting the two halves of the brain. Originally, this rather drastic-sounding treatment

was carried out, in the early 1960s, by Joseph Bogen of California to ease the pain of sufferers of extreme fits of epilepsy. By cutting the *corpus callosum* and the anterior commissure, another bunch of nerve fibres joining the two hemispheres of the brain, epileptic seizures were kept from spreading from one side to the other. The patients who underwent this surgery stopped having fits and in every respect appeared quite normal.

This fact was a source of puzzlement to neurophysiologists, because they could not understand why such major surgery apparently had no negative effects on the patients. Perhaps A. L. Wigan was right: perhaps, after all, humans did have two separate minds, and cutting the connecting links simply enhanced their independence.

However, it was not until R. W. Sperry and his colleagues at the California Institute of Technology started studying 'split-brain' effects in cats and monkeys and then extended their research to 'split-brain' humans that some curious anomalies in behaviour emerged. Sperry and his fellow researchers had reasoned that cutting the human *corpus callosum* meant that the speech and writing areas located in the dominant left hemisphere were no longer in contact with the right hemisphere that controlled the left side of the body. Therefore, they argued, if an object were presented in the left-hand side of the field of vision (which was perceived by the right hemisphere of the subject's brain), the 'split-brain' patients would be able to see the object, but could not explain what it was, nor write about it – these functions being a left-brain activity.

Sperry and his team set up a series of simple experiments to explore these ideas. In one such experiment, a split-brain patient sat on one side of a screen. Behind the screen, out of his view, was a collection of small, simple objects such as a hammer, a knife, a nut, a bolt, and so on. The name of

The 17th-century engraving, above, shows magicians in concert. Western society regards magic as 'sinister' – a word derived from the Latin for left-sided – perhaps because it apparently has no rational foundation.

In the carving below, the sacred boat of the Egyptian goddess Isis is seen sailing through the night. Processions in honour of Isis were traditionally led by priests bearing the image of a left hand.

The portrait by Jaco Bar, below, right, is of Fra Luca Pacioli, one of the great Renaissance geometers. In the western tradition, the analytical has always been favoured at the expense of the intuitive. But intuition can sometimes aid in the most analytical thought processes. The famous 19th-century French mathematician Henri Poincaré, below, for instance, made an important mathematical discovery apparently almost by accident: it came to him in a flash of intuition while he was not consciously thinking of the problem.

one object was flashed for one-tenth of a second on to the screen in such a way that it was recognised only by the right hemisphere. When the patient was asked to name the object, he failed; but if he felt behind the screen with his left hand, he selected the correct object.

Many other controlled scientific experiments on this theme have been carried out, together with investigations of brain activity using electroencephalographs to compare neural activity in the two hemispheres when the subject is carrying out a number of varied tasks.

There are of course, the artists, sculptors, mystics and people who 'drop out' of the system and counter this left-brain domination by trying to assert the value of right-brain activity but they still remain, in general, a barely tolerated minority on the fringes of our society. Nonetheless, their presence may indicate that they are the vanguard of a new form of consciousness – a consciousness that embraces both right-brain and left-brain thought and behaviour. But this new form of consciousness will have a difficult struggle if it is to counter the powerful forces that favour left-brain dominance. Bearing

The left brain controls speech, writing and numerical abilities; its mode of thought is analytical, logical, and rational; and it proceeds by rigorous step-by-step analysis of the problems it is set. The right hemisphere, meanwhile, controls the ability to visualise in three dimensions, a 'sense of direction' and musical ability; it is perceptual, intuitive, imaginative, and discerns things as wholes or in terms of patterns rather than by analysing them logically in the manner of the left hemisphere.

Such findings lead us to interesting conclusions. The reason why, for most people, the left hemisphere of the brain appears to be dominant, for instance, is that its abilities in the verbal, analytical and logical areas are those that are the most highly regarded – in western culture, at least. The mathematician is trained so that his left-brain functions are developed to a high degree, whereas the value of his right brain can go unnoticed until the left brain relaxes its hold over thought processes. Poincaré's insights, remember, came to him in a flash, demonstrating that the processes of his right brain were largely unconscious, coming to the fore when not actively called upon.

in mind that the left brain controls the right side of the body, we would expect that, under the regime of the old consciousness, right-sidedness would be favoured, while in certain cultures the left side would have a flavour of disrepute about it.

Evidence confirms this: *The Bible*, for instance, indicates that God 'shall set the sheep on his right hand, but the goats on his left' (*Matthew* 25:33). The goats are not only placed on the left: they are ultimately destined to be thrown to the Devil.

In the Greek tradition of Pythagoras – a patriarchal tradition – the right side was associated with the light and the Sun, the straight, the good and the male, whereas the left corresponded to the dark and the Moon, the crooked, the evil and the female. In ancient Egypt, however – a matriarchal society – the Isis cult honoured the female, Isis, rather than the male, Osiris. Night was revered rather than day, and the Isis processions were led by priests holding an image of the left hand.

Western society, with its patriarchal, male-dominated view of the world, inherited from the Greeks, has suppressed the matriarchal view of the Egyptians – and there seems little alternative but to

conclude that this is because a rival order constitutes a threat to the dominance of the right side.

It is perhaps significant that western society sees as *sinister* (from the Latin for 'left-sided') such activities as magic and mysticism, because there appears to be no rational logic behind them. But activities such as transcendental meditation, yoga, faith healing, parapsychology, divining and achieving altered states of consciousness through the use of drugs all defy left-brain logic, and are practised by increasing numbers of people.

The growth in the pursuit of these 'sinister' activities has arisen, it seems, because more and more people are rebelling and reacting against the alienation, depersonalisation and rationalisation imposed by western technological existence, and are seeking to let their right brains come alive, thereby restoring the balance between left and right brains. The right brain can be seen to be reasserting itself in all aspects of life, ranging from

A medieval wall painting from St Thomas' church, Salisbury, England, above, shows the Last Judgement. Souls who are to go to heaven are sitting at God's right hand; those who are doomed to perdition are on his left.

The Tarot card designed for Aleister Crowley by Frieda Harris, right, features the interlocking symbols of yin and yang – the female and male principles, the integration of which represents the whole of existence. Yin and yang also broadly delineate the characteristics of the right and left brains respectively.

▟▟ INFORMATION COMES TO US SOMETIMES IN A FLASH, IN NO MORE TIME THAN IT TAKES TO DRAW A BREATH, TO HAVE AN INSPIRATION . . . IT CAN BE TRIGGERED BY MEDITATION, DEEP PRAYER, FASTING . . . BUT AT ITS BEST IT IS SPONTANEOUS. IT JUST ARRIVES OUT OF THE BLUE, SLIDING INTO CONSCIOUSNESS WHEN ONE LEAST EXPECTS IT. ▟▟

LYALL WATSON, SUPERNATURE II

an increasing willingness to take paranormal occurrences seriously to an interest in mystical systems.

If this rebellion by the right brain is to generate a new consciousness of life, it is important to keep a sense of perspective. What is necessary is not left- or right-brain dominance, but harmony between the two hemispheres of the brain. This harmony can arise only through an open dialogue between the halves of the brain, each contributing its own strengths and abilities. To this end, we may be able to train ourselves to use our right brains more consciously through, for example, biofeedback, giving time – from school age onwards – to 'right-brain' activities, and training ourselves to realise when to 'let go' or forget a problem so that the right brain can help to resolve it.

The renowned physicist Albert Einstein, it seems, was well practised in this. During his most enlightened moments, he seemed to relax and then allow his mind to wander, thinking in symbols rather than in words and sentences. Indeed, it is believed by some that the very use of language somehow imposes logic and thereby restricts potential creativity.

We may also be able to learn from the Chinese, who have long held the view that all existence is represented by the integration of opposites known as *yin,* the female principle, and *yang,* the male principle – opposites that also, broadly, delineate the contrast between the right and left brains. The philosophers of ancient China, it seems, were wiser than we are: they knew – centuries before western neurophysiologists began to discover the same truth – that without this active union of opposites we are, to put it simply, but half-brained.

THE ART OF MASS MIND CONTROL

ACCORDING TO ONE OF THE MOST DISTURBING RUMOURS TO ARISE IN THE LATE 20TH CENTURY, THE SOVIETS NOT ONLY MASTERED THE ART OF MASS MIND CONTROL, BUT ACTUALLY SET ABOUT USING IT

American psychic Shawn Robbins, right, revealed that the US Navy once invited her to take part in a project similar to Stanford Research Institute's remote viewing experiments. There is some evidence that many other psychics have also been approached by their governments as potential subjects in large-scale ESP experiments.

Astral espionage; subliminal propaganda by telepathy; thought-moulding of Western leaders; bioenergy as an anti-personnel weapon; knocking out military equipment and space vehicles with psychokinesis – these are not jottings from a science-fiction writer's notebook but some of the techniques solemnly discussed in two reports compiled in 1972 and 1975 for the US

The early warning station, below, is designed to detect incoming missiles. But what warning would we have if an enemy state chose to direct weapons of mind control against us?

Defense Intelligence Agency (DIA) under the titles *Controlled Offensive Behavior – USSR* and *Soviet and Czechoslovak Parapsychology Research*. The former was scheduled for declassification only in 1990, but was released under the Freedom of Information Act. While parts of the documents may strain the credulity of even the most avid of science fiction fans, a study of them in conjunction with other published information points to the very real possibility that the Third World War was well under way by the mid 1970s – and that the West was slowly losing it.

According to the DIA reports, the Soviets had a start of several decades over the West in officially funded research into psychic phenomena, especially telepathy, and their top priority was always its practical application. In other words, while the West was holding psychical research at arm's length, or even arguing it out of existence, the Soviets were looking for – and finding – ways of making telepathy and psychokinesis (PK) work for them.

Psychic Warfare

However, a 1976 report (allegedly funded by one of the US intelligence agencies) was more cautious. Surveying the published literature on what its authors term 'novel biophysical information transfer' (NBIT) – comprising both telepathy and PK – it concluded that, although most published material was 'confusing, inaccurate and of little value from a scientific point of view', there was good reason to suppose that secret *psi* research was indeed going on in the Soviet Union, and that the results were intended to be used by the military and secret police. One of the authors of the report was later quoted as saying: 'I believe the Soviets are actually building prototype equipment for psychic warfare.'

It became known in 1980, thanks to successful use of the Freedom of Information Act by US journalist Randy Fitzgerald, that the Central Intelligence Agency's involvement in psychic matters could be traced back at least to 1952.

In a CIA document dated 7 January of that year, the remarkable claim was made that: 'It looks as if... the problem of getting and maintaining control over the ESP function has been solved.' It was also recommended that 'suitable subjects' should be trained and put to work as psychic spies. A well-known American psychic, Shawn Robbins, later revealed that she had been invited to take part in a US Navy project along the lines of the remote viewing experiments carried out at Stanford Research Institute (SRI) with researchers Ingo Swann and Pat Price.

Then, early in 1981, psychic warfare made headlines in the USA when columnist Jack Anderson announced that the Pentagon had been maintaining its own secret 'psychic task force' since 1976. 'The brass hats,' he said, 'are indeed dabbling in the dark arts.' Anderson does not seem to have taken the activities of what he calls 'the voodoo warriors' very seriously; yet by a curious coincidence, the first of his two columns appeared just after a much more thoroughly researched piece on psychotronic warfare in *Military Review*, the professional journal of the US Army.

The article, entitled *The New Mental Battlefield*, was humorously subtitled 'Beam me up, Spock', a reference to the TV series, *Star Trek*. But there was nothing funny in the eight-page text, written by Lieutenant-Colonel J.B. Alexander, a holder of three university degrees who had clearly done his homework. Psychotronic research had been under way for years, he wrote, and its potential use in weaponry had been explored. 'To be more specific,' he went on, 'there are weapons systems that operate on the power of the mind and whose lethal capacity has already been demonstrated.' After a candid and open-minded survey of his subject, he admitted that some would find it ridiculous 'since it does not conform to their view of reality'. However, he added, 'some people still believe the world is flat', and he called for more co-ordinated research into the paranormal, recommending that leaders at all levels should be provided with 'a basic understanding of weapons systems they may encounter in the not-too-distant future'.

Some indication of just what these weapons might be was given by Thomas E. Bearden, a retired US Army officer with long experience in nuclear engineering, war games analysis and air defence systems. He described a terrifying arsenal of some 26 devices, ranging from machines that modify the weather and broadcast 'disease patterns' to the 'hyperspace nuclear howitzer' and even an earthquake generator. Bearden uses quantum mechanics and Jungian psychology to build a model of psychotronic reality that is unlikely to conform to the views of many, although Lyall Watson, who discusses Bearden's theories in his book *Lifetide*, finds some of his ideas 'horribly plausible' and senses 'a rightness in his approach'.

But before the psychotronic scenario gets even more bizarre, two questions must be asked: who is winning the *psi* arms race, and is there any real evidence that any *psi* weaponry has ever been used?

According to Richard Deacon, author of several studies of international espionage, the first country to take the lead in *psi* warfare techniques could achieve 'something like total superiority'. And, he pointed out, the country with the most active interest in and best information on the subject is neither

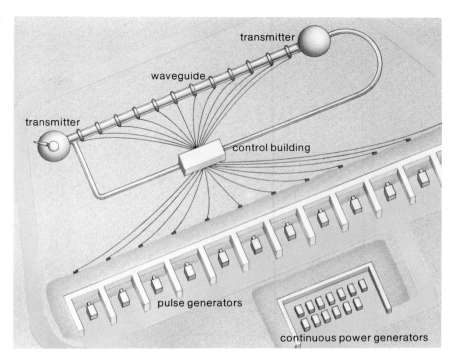

P E R S P E C T I V E S

A PAWN IN THEIR GAME

Anatoli Karpov, Soviet grand master, and Viktor Korchnoi, the Soviet defector, are seen below during their intense battle of wits at the 1978 World Chess Championship at Baguio City in the Philippines.

Who really won the 1978 World Chess Championship – Soviet grand master Anatoli Karpov, Soviet defector Viktor Korchnoi, or a mysterious man named Dr Vladimir Zukhar? According to the record books, it was the seemingly unflappable Karpov who retained his title after winning five games out of the first six, losing the next four, and finally returning to form and sweeping the board.

Korchnoi thought otherwise. Dr Zukhar, he alleged, was a psychic saboteur sent to the Philippines to make sure that Karpov avoided losing to a defector.

Korchnoi obviously believed that psychic powers could affect his game, for he took countermeasures of his own, in the form of training in yoga and meditation from two American members of the Anand Marg sect who happened to be in town. They also taught him a Sanskrit mantra to ward off evil, which he claimed to have used against Zukhar with devastating effect.

This was not the first time psychic matters had been raised at a world chess tournament. Interestingly, it was the Soviets who cried foul play at the 1972 confrontation between Bobby Fischer and Boris Spassky, suggesting not only that Fischer's chair was wired to receive messages from accomplices, but that Fischer, or at any rate somebody, was actually trying to cast an evil spell over Spassky. And at the world title elimination bout in 1977, Spassky had part of the stage screened off, so that he could hide from both Korchnoi and the audience. The former was paralysing his mind, he said, while the latter were beaming rays at him.

Could Dr Zukhar have helped Karpov win in 1978? By then, the Soviets had more than 50 years of state-backed research in telepathy to draw on; and if scientists in the 1920s could broadcast suggestions that subjects should scratch their noses, it seems possible that Zukhar could make Korchnoi move the wrong pawn at the wrong time.

'Chess is almost the perfect game for PK effects to make a real difference,' commented Dr Carl Sargent, a parapsychologist and chess enthusiast. 'One lapse of concentration may mean the blunder which costs the game or even the match.' A feature of the Korchnoi-Karpov games was indeed the number lost by apparent mistakes rather than won by skill.

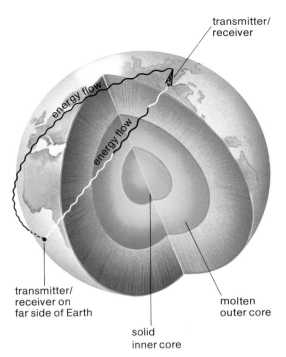

transmitter/
receiver

transmitter/
receiver on
far side of Earth

energy flow

energy flow

solid
inner core

molten
outer core

of the so-called 'superpowers', but Israel. Quoting intelligence sources, Deacon stated that the Israelis have first-hand knowledge of military *psi* research in seven Russian cities and at least four Eastern European countries. One of Israel's most alarming claims, according to Deacon, is that the Soviets were working in the mid 1970s on 'subliminal conditioning' by telepathy, through 'transference of behaviour impulses'. So has telepathic mind control already been put into practice?

In 1976, one possible means by which this could have been done became public knowledge. In that year, a number of new Soviet radio stations went on the air, mystifying listeners around the world by confining their programme content to a loud and steady rattle. One of these stations, at Gomel (near Minsk), was believed to have 20 times the peak output of any previously known transmitter. The Soviet 'woodpecker' (which is what it sounded like) was splashing across several frequencies on the short-wave band and was even interfering with telephones.

RADIO DISRUPTION

Telecommunications companies, amateur radio societies and several governments complained to the Soviet Union. The Soviets apologised, saying they were carrying out 'experiments' and promised to minimise disruption. But they never explained what they were doing, and early guesses were that they were working on a new form of over-the-horizon radar. Then, in 1977, the American psychical investigator Andrija Puharich startled a London audience with a detailed account of what he believed was really going on.

The Soviets, Puharich said, had put into practice an idea originally thought up by the scientific genius Nikola Tesla (1857-1943) around the turn of the century, and were using their transmitters to set up a colossal stationary wave passing through the core of the Earth and carrying a signal tuned to resonate with the Earth-atmosphere system. This signal was

being pulsed in the extremely low frequency (ELF) band, at 4 to 15 pulses per second, a range of special importance to the human brain, and comprising the theta and alpha bands.

In laboratory experiments, Puharich found that brain rhythms fell into step with whatever frequency in these bands was being beamed at them, even when the subject was in a shielded metal Faraday cage. Fine tuning of the pulse rate could also produce a wide range of symptoms, from tension headaches and nausea to drowsiness. This sinister process of 'bioentrainment' was, he claimed, being tried out on a country especially selected for the Soviet 'experiment' – Canada.

This was not all. Puharich claimed that ways had been found to get the psychotronic effect, in the form of a telepathic signal, on to the woodpecker signal. Something like this had been specifically predicted in detail by the authors of the 1976 report. So, fantastic as it may seem, it is an idea that has occurred to others besides Puharich. Indeed, it has often been noted that the physicist Dr Ippolit M. Kogan put forward a hypothesis in the 1960s on the use of ELF waves as carriers of telepathy and that, after 1969, Kogan's name completely disappeared from the published literature. Western observers also noticed that any accounts of psychical research published by the Soviets after 1970 described old, well-known experiments, as if their real work in this field had suddenly been deemed top secret.

" FIGHTING IS THE MOST PRIMITIVE

WAY OF MAKING WAR ON YOUR

ENEMIES. THE SUPREME

EXCELLENCE IS TO SUBDUE THE

ARMIES OF YOUR ENEMIES WITHOUT

HAVING TO FIGHT THEM. *"*

SUN TZU, EARLY 4TH CENTURY BC

INTELLIGENT SPECIES

ANCIENT THINKERS VIEWED ANIMALS AS BEING CUNNING, WISE OR INGENIOUS; AND FOLKLORE ABOUNDS WITH TALES OF ANIMAL CLEVERNESS. HERE, WE TAKE A LOOK AT RESEARCH INTO THEIR SPECIFIC ABILITIES

Almost 200 years ago, the *Daily Universal Register* (forerunner of *The Times*) advertised a curious evening entertainment: a performance by the 'amazing learned pig'. This 'entertaining and sagacious animal', so readers were assured: 'casts accounts by means of Typographical cards, in the same manner as a Printer composes; and by the same method sets down any Capital or Surname, reckons the number of People present, tells by evoking [sic] on a Gentleman's Watch in company what is the Hour and Minutes; he likewise tells any Lady's thoughts in company, and distinguishes any sort of colours.'

There were many other 'learned pigs' advertised by showmen in the 18th and 19th centuries; and,

For centuries, performing animals delighted crowds with what seemed to be feats of reasoning. In Elizabethan England, a bay gelding called Morocco, below right, for instance, had a large stock of tricks. When a silver coin was presented to him, he could even indicate how many pence were equivalent to it and earned a mention by Shakespeare in Love's Labour's Lost. *Two hundred years later, the 'Surprising Pig', below, was showing itself to be 'well versed in all languages' and a 'perfect Arithmatician, Mathematician and Composer of Musick'. But it is probably safe to say that the feats of these performing animals were nothing more than tricks – responses that they had been trained to make to cues from their owners.*

although few were credited with the alarming ability to read 'any Lady's thoughts', all of them were a source of wonder to the general populace. But 18th- and 19th-century 'natural philosophers' were not impressed. Such a pig, they said, was merely performing tricks taught by its master. When, for example, a 'learned pig' was presented with the printed numbers 5 and 8 and indicated their total by making 13 taps with one of its trotters, it was doing no more than obeying subtle signals that were given by its owner.

In this assertion, the 'natural philosophers' were certainly right. But, curiously enough, the argument that led them to this conclusion was equally certainly wrong. Intelligence, they believed, was a purely human attribute, and it distinguished Man from the lower animals: the 'brute creation' was incapable of reasoning, all its spontaneous activities being the product of blind instinct. Those men and women, they said, who produced anecdotal evidence of animal intelligence – a pet cat learning how to unlatch and open a door, for example – were confusing reason with its very opposite, blind trial and error.

The first real challenge to this ancient Man-centred theory of intelligence, formulated by Aristotle over 2,000 years ago, came from Charles Darwin. In *The Descent of Man*, he argued that animal

behaviour indicated not only instinct but 'some power of reasoning.' The difference between the minds of men and those of higher animals, he wrote, 'great as it is, is certainly one of degree and not kind.

Darwin's assertion did not meet with unqualified assent, however. It was 'anecdotal' – based, it was true, on close observation, but lacking laboratory evidence. What was needed, it was said, was controlled experimentation.

Two students of animal behaviour, Edward Lee Thorndike, an American, and Wolfgang Köhler, a German, carried out such experiments. Their results, and the conclusions they drew from them, seemed curiously conflicting. Thorndike, working from the 1890s onwards, found that the animals he experimented with solved problems by pure trial and error, showing no insight into the real nature of the problem before them, but simply blundering about until sometimes, purely by accident, they found a solution. If, for example, cats or monkeys were put in closed containers, they made random attempts to get free, persisting until they either became exhausted or, by chance, managed to find the escape mechanism.

Köhler used chimpanzees as his subjects in a famous series of experiments conducted from 1913 to 1920. And he found that his animals solved problems in a way that he regarded as evidence of insight. If, for example, bananas or other chimpanzee delicacies were hung out of reach of his subjects, the animals would get at them by constructing a makeshift ladder of boxes piled on top of one another. Similarly, they would use a bamboo pole to rake in food placed well outside their cages: if the food was placed too far away to be reached with one bamboo, they would fit one pole into the cavity of another in order to make a longer rake.

NATIONAL CHARACTERISTICS

These conflicting results attracted the derision of renowned philosopher Bertrand Russell, who jokingly claimed that the experimental animals were reflecting the national characteristics of their observers. 'Animals studied by Americans,' he wrote, 'rush about frantically, with an incredible display of hustle and pep, and at last achieve the desired result by chance. Animals observed by Germans sit still and think, and at last evolve the solution out of their inner consciousness.'

In fact, there was no real conflict between the results of the two experimental series. As Köhler pointed out, Thorndike had presented his monkeys and other animals with problems that could be solved *only* by trial and error: the escape mechanism of his boxes was hidden from view, so his subjects could not use any capacity of insight they may have possessed. This meant that the only way they could get free was to blunder about.

But Köhler's results have also been criticized, on the grounds that, if chimpanzees are not previously acquainted with bamboos, and have never been given them to play with, they do not use one as a food rake when first presented with it. This, it has been argued, shows 'lack of insight' – 'insight' here means the ability to solve a problem by thinking about it and then acting, rather than by blind trial and error.

But this kind of reasoning seems beside the point. Clearly, if a chimpanzee has lacked the opportunity to experiment with bamboo sticks by playing with them, it will be unacquainted with many of their properties – for example, with the fact that, by careful manipulation, the end of one can be inserted into the cavity of another. It is therefore unable to employ any possible powers of insight that it might possess in relation to the bamboo's use as a tool.

A useful analogy would be to imagine an intelligent primitive man being locked into a cage and then presented with a key. Not having any knowledge of the general properties of locks and keys, it would be most unlikely that any insight on his part would enable him to discover the use of the key: he would be forced to use trial and error in his efforts to escape.

What Köhler's chimpanzees had done was essentially the same as what human beings do when engaged in thought – they applied relevant past experience to a new situation. On this level, at least, there seems to be something in common between animal and human intelligence.

TOOL-USERS

What, then, is the essential difference between Man and other animals? Is there, indeed, such a difference? One traditional definition of Man is that he is the only animal capable of using tools. But, as we have seen, Köhler's chimpanzees actually manufactured simple tools – by fitting two bamboos together to make rakes – when it served their purposes. There can be no question of this tool-using faculty being a mere imitation of human activities witnessed by the chimpanzees, for Köhler was careful never to use sticks as a means of raking while he was anywhere in the neighbourhood of his laboratory. In any case, chimpanzees and other simians in the wild have been observed to use sticks as tools.

In one of Wolfgang Köhler's classic experiments, top, food was placed just outside a chimpanzee's enclosure. Bamboo sticks were available, but they were too short to reach the food. After an hour of trying to reach the food with them, the chimp, Sultan, gave up. Then, playing with two sticks, he happened to slot one into the other. Immediately, he rushed off and used them to pull in the food. Chimps also use sticks as tools in their natural surroundings. One, top right, gets at termites by thrusting a stick into their nest, and then lifting the stick to his mouth and licking off the termites clinging to it. Chimpanzee thought processes can be probed by IQ tests, above. Here, the subject, scratching its chin as if puzzled, has to match shapes.

For example, chimpanzees regard termites as highly desirable items of diet. The problem is to get at the termites, which live underground in gigantic nests resembling those of ants. The chimpanzees have solved the problem by utilizing sticks. These are thrust into the nest, and the infuriated termites attack them and crawl all over them. The monkeys then pull out the sticks and lick off their longed-for delicacy.

Interestingly enough, sticks are also used to get at termites in a radically different way by another large group of chimpanzees, biologically identical, but living far away. This second group uses the sticks as tools to break open the termite nests: but then they will use their hands to scoop up the termites. It seems probable that, in each group, some monkey of genius first discovered the use of sticks as a means of getting at termites, and that this discovery was eventually observed and imitated by its fellows. Alternatively, it is a remote but exciting possibility that the discovery was originally made in only one of the groups and was 'transmitted' in slightly garbled form to the other group by means of the kind of 'morphogenetic field' posited by Dr Rupert Sheldrake.

CHANGING PATTERNS

However, even if this were the case, it seems certain that, within the group in which the original discovery was made, transmission from the genius chimpanzee to its fellows was by means of observation and imitation, for similar cultural transmission has been reported in monkeys observed over many years living in semi-wild conditions. Thus, a tribe of rhesus macaques, living under wild but controlled conditions in Japan, was observed to make a fundamental change in its feeding pattern as the result of a discovery made by just one talented female.

" COMMUNICATION SIGNALS BETWEEN ANIMALS HAVE BEEN SHOWN, DURING THE PAST THIRTY YEARS, TO BE COMPLEX, DIVERSE AND VERSATILE, BEYOND WHAT WAS PREVIOUSLY EXPECTED. **"**

PETER REDGROVE, THE BLACK GODDESS AND THE SIXTH SENSE

The Japanese macaque monkeys that wash sweet potatoes in the sea or a stream, *above*, before eating them, first learned this novelty from a particular female who decided that the taste of her food was improved by this process. That her new-fangled ways should spread through the whole of her group is not particularly

MONKEY BUSINESS

surprising; but what is remarkable is that soon afterwards, it was reported that macaque monkeys on other islands had begun to wash their food in water in exactly the same way.

There are several alternative explanations for this. It is possible, though hardly likely, that someone transported individual monkeys from the foodwashing group to other islands. It is even possible that some form of animal telepathy was involved. But the most exciting explanation is provided by Rupert Sheldrake's hypothesis of 'morphogenesis'. According to this theory, both physical and biological processes are promoted if similar processes have occurred in the past. One aspect of this is that animals of a particular species are able to draw on that species' 'memory bank'. Once one group of macaques had acquired the new habit of washing their food, the trick would become easier for other macaques, even in remote places, to use.

PERSPECTIVES

Sweet potatoes are an important part of the diet of these monkeys. A certain amount of dirt and small stones clings to them when the monkeys dig them out of the soil. For a long time, all the monkeys seemed to accept the inconvenience of eating a certain amount of dirt as being in the nature of things; but, eventually, a young female, more fastidious and more intelligent than her companions, took to carefully washing her sweet potatoes in the sea before eating them. There is no doubt that she really was washing them, not just adding salt to her diet, because after a time she began to carry out the process in streams of fresh water. At first, her behaviour was imitated only by her close companions, young monkeys whose minds were clearly open to radical innovations. But, in time, the new pre-feeding rituals spread through the entire group. The last to adopt it were the older adult males, as culturally conservative as their human equivalents,

who slowly, and doubtless with much grumbling, may have decided they had to move with the times.

If, then, animals can innovate and use tools, and are capable of insight, perhaps it is the use of language that separates Man from other animals? Such a view has long been advocated – in fact, language has been characterized as 'a distinctly human attribute'.

CONVEYING INFORMATION

There is a certain amount of truth in this: while all animals have some mode of conveying information to their fellows – sometimes of great complexity, as in the 'dance language' of honey bees – no species other than Man has a language in the sense of a flexible range of sounds or gestures, with an extendible syntax, capable of conveying abstract ideas. Nevertheless, some species use sounds in a way that is analogous to the words of a very simple language – for example, to symbolize objects that are not present. The velvet monkeys that live in southern Kenya provide a good example of this type of animal communication.

The vervets seem to have four main enemies: eagles, particularly the martial eagle; snakes, particularly the python; baboons; and, most deadly of all, leopards. For each of these predatory groups, the vervets have been shown to use a separate warning sound – a 'word' – and their response to one 'word' is quite different from their response to another. If the 'word' for leopard is screamed by an observant monkey, all the vervets climb trees, going out on branches that are too thin to support the predator. If, on the other hand, the signal for 'eagle' is given, the vervets avoid trees and instead hide in thick undergrowth. The words for 'baboon' and 'snake' evoke still different responses. In response to the first, the vervets move away as a group; in response to the second, they all stand on tiptoe, peering at the ground until they locate the snake and then move away from it.

These warning sounds have at least one thing in common with language. They are in no way innate,

Symbols on the chimp's computer keyboard, above, represent words. By pressing several keys in sequence, she can form simple sentences.

The vervet monkeys, left, take refuge after hearing another monkey give the alarm call for 'leopard'. Vervets have been shown to use different calls – or 'words' – for different enemies.

genetically programmed signals, such as the lowing of a cow or the snorting of a pig. Young monkeys have to learn them from their elders, in much the same way as human infants acquire their vocabulary. And, just as human children sometimes use the wrong word, so do vervets. It may sometimes, in error, give the signal for an eagle when a pigeon flies by; or, much worse, it can get the entire tribe on tiptoe, looking for snakes, when the real threat comes from an approaching baboon.

EXPERIMENTAL TEACHING

It has been suggested that some animals with highly developed brains, such as chimpanzees, have failed to develop and use language in any way, not because they are incapable of doing so, but rather because they had no evolutionary need to do so. In order to test this hypothesis, various attempts have been made by experimenters working in this field to teach individual chimpanzees a language of some kind.

The first such experiment, an attempt to teach a young chimpanzee to speak English, was a failure. After much effort, the animal acquired a vocabulary of four types of grunt, which were only just recognizable as somewhat unsatisfactory attempts to pronounce English words. This result was exactly what could have been expected – the larynx of a chimpanzee is mechanically incapable of producing the right sort of sounds.

Later experiments were far more encouraging. A female chimpanzee, named Washoe, was brought up by an American couple who treated her almost exactly like a human child, save that they never spoke in her presence; instead, they communicated with one another in Ameslan, a sign language that is widely used in the United States by the deaf and dumb. Remarkably, Washoe acquired a vocabulary of 160 Ameslan words. Some of these she was taught by the experimenters; others, more interestingly, she picked up as a result of observing the gestures of her human 'parents'. Even more extraordinary, Washoe began to string signs together in

order to express more complex concepts. Thus, she spontaneously made the sign for 'bird' and the sign for 'water' when she first saw a swan. On one occasion, she was taken on an outing and saw some caged animals. Her comment on these seems to have indicated both thought and emotion; 'animals unhappy' was what she gestured to her 'parents'.

On coming to maturity, Washoe was moved to a centre for the study of primates. Several of her fellows also learned the sign language and used it to communicate with one another. One of them, a male called Ally, not only learned to understand simple spoken words, but actually managed to translate them into Ameslan gestures for the benefit of his companions.

Another chimpanzee, Sarah, was taught an artificial language in which coloured plastic chips of varying shape represented a total of 13 English nouns, adjectives and verbs. Soon, she came to understand simple sentences spelt out to her in this form. For example, when she was presented with a series of chips meaning 'Sarah put apple pail Sarah put banana dish', she duly put an apple in her pail, and a banana in her dish. Clearly, this chimpanzee had learned not just a vocabulary, but also the rudiments of syntax.

This ability to obey a command, never before encountered, suggests an ability to conceive of a not-yet-existent state of affairs. And the ability to make and understand utterances that have never been explicitly taught to the animal is far removed from the simple stimulus-response behaviour that makes up so much of mental activity. Such remarkable behaviour certainly deserves to be regarded as demonstrating simple language abilities on the part of chimpanzees.

At the end of the 20th century, language research with chimpanzees is still at an early stage. But there are definite indications that it may ultimately revolutionize both our conception of animal intelligence and, perhaps, our understanding of the nature of language itself.

Nim Chimpsky, a great chimpanzee linguist, below, was taught to use sign language to 'say' that he wants to play with the cat. In the first three pictures, reading from the left, he uses the sign sequence 'me hug cat'. Then Nim gets his wish!

For years on end, a young American woman called Ruth, living in London, was afflicted by hostile hallucinations of her father, who lived on the other side of the Atlantic at the time. These hallucinations affected her senses of sight, hearing, smell and touch. Indeed, it was almost as if her father had been constantly physically present. Ruth thought she was going mad; but, through the treatment of a wise psychiatrist, she learned that her ability to fantasize was in its way a gift that she could – and did – develop for positive use. She was, unwittingly, what is known as a fantasy-prone personality, and the late developer of a talent that some fortunate people, perhaps 3 or 4 per cent of the population, possess all their lives.

There have been several studies into the nature of such personalities. Dr Sheryl C. Wilson and Dr Theodore X. Barber, both of Cushing Hospital, Framingham, Massachusetts, USA, for instance, tested 27 female fantasy-prone personalities together with a control group of 25 'normal' women. The fantasy-prone women were selected on the grounds of their extremely positive responses to certain standard psychological tests in guided imagining, hypnosis and suggestibility, and to other tests devised by the experimenters. With two exceptions, every member of the group was university educated. Their ages ranged from 19 to 63 years, with a mean of 28. All but four, in the experimenters' estimation, were either socially normal or exceptionally well-adjusted: the remainder, of whom one had been through a nervous breakdown, faced difficulties such as depression. Twenty-four had husbands or relationships with one or more boyfriends. It cannot be over-emphasized that, aside from their genius for fantasizing, the fantasy-prone women were perfectly normal people. They were, so to speak, at one extreme end of a curve representing a certain kind of ability. Otherwise, they were quite ordinary – just as a mathematician, artist or musician, exceptionally talented in his or her field, may be entirely ordinary in everything else.

The abilities of fantasy-prone people, Wilson and Barber found, generally begin in childhood. Many of them – like many sensitives – had childhood playmates as real as flesh-and-blood companions whom, as they sometimes learned through bitter experience, adults could not see. Not only this, they

THE FANTASY-PRONE

MOST OF US DREAM ONLY WHILE WE ARE ASLEEP.

BUT THERE ARE SOME WHO SEEM TO LIVE IN A CURIOUS

WORLD OF FANTASY MOST OF THE TIME

The genius for fantasizing is, in many ways, a gift that can be put to positive use. There is, for instance, a remarkable similarity between The Temptation of St Anthony, *from the Isenheim altarpiece by Mathias Grunewald (c.1460-1528), above, and a painting by a drug addict showing visions experienced as withdrawal symptoms, right.*
Dr Sheryl C. Wilson, top, and Dr Theodore X. Barber, above, of Cushing Hospital, Framingham, Massachusetts, USA, both investigated the experiences of fantasy-prone personalities.

often 'became' characters from books they read, ceasing to be themselves in a way that is perhaps similar to that in which a great actor loses himself completely in the character he portrays. Fantasies are not without danger: a child who believed she was leading a lamb through a meadow, for instance, suddenly 'awoke' to find herself alone, surrounded by traffic in a city street.

A consciously developed ability to fantasize can also continue into adult life for a number of reasons. Adults significant to the child may provide encouragement through accepting the child's viewpoint supportively, and convincingly, as their own. A child may also use his fantasy world to escape from isolation, loneliness, a deprived or distressing environment or a particular activity that he dislikes, such as intensive piano practice.

SECRET TALENTS

Realisation that they are not like others in their fantasizing ability frequently makes the adult fantasy-prone individuals somewhat secretive about their talents. Consequently, they share their secrets with no one, not even their marital partners. Some, however, actually find relief in fantasizing during contact with strangers, pretending to be characters other than themselves.

Interestingly, fantasy-prone people often have psychic abilities above the average; and the 27 women in the Massachusetts experiment were found to be gifted in telepathy, precognition (waking and in dreams), premonitions (one subject forecast the Kentucky Derby winners for 10 years in succession but did not back them because she considered this a misuse of her faculty), psychometry, mediumistic trances, perception of the presence of spirits, encounters with apparitions (one apparition revealed to one of the subjects the existence of a missing will), 'seeing' people's thoughts in images above their heads, dowsing, automatic writing (felt

Fantasy-prone people often 'become' characters from books they read or films they see, ceasing to be themselves in a similar way to that in which great actors lose themselves in the characters they portray – just as Richard Burton did in the stage version of Camelot, *above, for example.*

to come from an entity outside the subject), and the capacity to affect the working of electrical appliances. Twenty-two subjects reported out-of-the-body experiences, while two claimed to carry out healing, and a third to minister to the dying during astral travel.

Like other psychics, fantasy-prone people have vivid imaginations. They do not merely recall events but relive them with the sights, smells, sounds, tactile impressions and emotions of the original experiences. Many of them also have a perfect auditory memory. Their recollections, like their fantasies, are in many ways similar to films – but films that they not only watch, but in which they play a part. Some fantasy-prone people are also able to eliminate unpleasant memories through amnesia. However, they have a tendency to confuse fantasy memories with memories of actual events.

TRANSPORTS OF DELIGHT

Fantasy-prone people live an outwardly normal life – but many of them admit to spending more than half their lives in a fantasy existence. In social contacts, they can fantasize about what is being discussed or described by their companions, or use fantasy to escape from boredom. They often react intensely to stimuli – a passing mention of Egypt, for example, can transport them to a pharaoh's court or to modern Alexandria. They can fly from routine or unpleasant experiences into a holiday world, a 'previous life', a trip into the future, travel to other galaxies or enjoy a sexual experience with a fantastic lover, who can give them greater orgasmic satisfaction than any live human being.

In idle moments, or while preparing for sleep, they can surrender to fantasy, set the stage, create the plot and characters and then sit back, as it were, to watch the play unfold. One third of subjects found it better to watch their 'home movies' with closed eyes; but to two-thirds, it did not matter whether

Many fantasy-prone women have reported phantom pregnancies, and some have even sought abortions. In Edward Albee's play Who's Afraid of Virginia Woolf?, *Honey, above, – played by Sandy Dennis – is a plain country girl whose husband married her because of a phantom pregnancy.*

The medium Mrs Ena Twigg, left, like many fantasy-prone people, had imaginary childhood playmates whom she was startled to realise others could not see.

their eyes were open or shut. All the subjects, however, reported that they experienced their fantasies with all their senses as real events. To all fantasy-prone people, 'real' life is a shadow of their fantasy existence. To be deprived of the latter would be, to them, a living death too terrible to contemplate.

DANGEROUS DAYDREAMS

But there are dangers and inconveniences associated with fantasies for adults, too. The fantasy of a child running on to a road from behind a parked car may make a driver brake suddenly and cause an accident, and fantasy-prone drivers have sometimes to try hard not to fantasize. Physical symptoms, even actual illnesses, may result from fantasies. Thirteen out of 22 women questioned in the Massachusetts project admitted having had at least one false pregnancy. Each had experienced several symptoms of the condition, and two had even sought abortions.

Another of the talents exhibited by many fantasy-prone people is the control of their autonomic bodily functions – heart rate, blood pressure, skin temperature and so on. They have the ability to feel hot or cold at will, a faculty that leads to the consideration that they may be practising some form of

An early seance-room photograph, left, shows a medium and her spirit guide. Many fantasy-prone people have psychic gifts. It has even been suggested that spirits may be mass hallucinations of their fantasies.

self-hypnosis. Fantasy-prone people tend to make excellent hypnotic subjects. It has also been found that many of them respond well to suggestions of age regression and to visual and auditory hallucinations. They react well to negative hallucinations, too – that is, suggestions that something or someone who is actually present is not there. They can, however, if they wish, refuse to cooperate with a hypnotist and are able to ignore any therapeutic suggestions made by him or her.

Well over half the 27 women in the experiment frequently experienced hypnopompic and hypnagogic visions – that is, extremely realistic and vivid hallucinations seen in the states intermediate between sleeping and waking, and waking and sleeping. But they felt these to be different from their deliberately created fantasies and were relieved and grateful to know that they were not unusual in this.

The experiences of such fantasy-prone people are certainly significant for psychical research. Study of their characteristics may throw light on mediums, for example. Indeed, it is possible that some spirit guides and communications are actually created by subconscious fantasizing. Their experiences also challenge the nature of our very perception of reality, which we assume communicates itself, by stimulation of the senses, in approximately the same way to everyone experiencing it. Perhaps there is indeed another, inner or 'mirror' reality, that communicates in a different way. And just as the average person is ordinarily unaware of psychical phenomena, yet has perhaps one or two experiences of them during the course of his life, so perhaps he may have, very rarely, a momentary revelation of the fantasy-prone person's inner reality, in which he experiences an hallucination as real. The knowledge that there are personalities who constantly have such experiences may thus help the ordinary man or woman to come to terms with such a one-off event.

P E R S P E C T I V E S

COMING DOWN TO EARTH

Barber and Wilson's experiments revealed that most of their subjects could be labelled without exaggeration as 'fantasy addicts'. Of 17 subjects asked to estimate what proportion of the day they spent in fantasy, 11 estimated it to be over 90 per cent. In fact, they found it easier to estimate the amount of time during which they did not fantasize. One said that she tried consciously to refrain from it while she was driving, but that otherwise she fantasized all the time. But although she fantasized vividly with all her senses, this did not affect her ability to function normally in the real world.

The women studied in the experiment had some interesting stories to tell about their childhood. As a rule, they had spent all their time fantasizing and could not tell their fantasy worlds from the real world. One remembered her bewilderment when she was finally convinced that Santa Claus did not exist: she could not understand why adults should want to 'make him up', when all around there were real magical beings, such as elves, fairies and tree spirits.

Other subjects reported how they would pretend to be other people – orphans, princesses, animals or birds – and would become utterly engrossed in the role they were playing. One woman described how she had believed, not that she was pretending to be a princess, but that she was a princess pretending to be an ordinary little girl. She was brought back down to earth with a jolt when she took some of her school-friends home to see the magnificent castle she had described to them as her home. They, of course, seeing only the middle-class house that was actually there, accused her of lying. She could not believe that they could not see the castle: to her, it was more real than the world that her friends insisted was genuine.

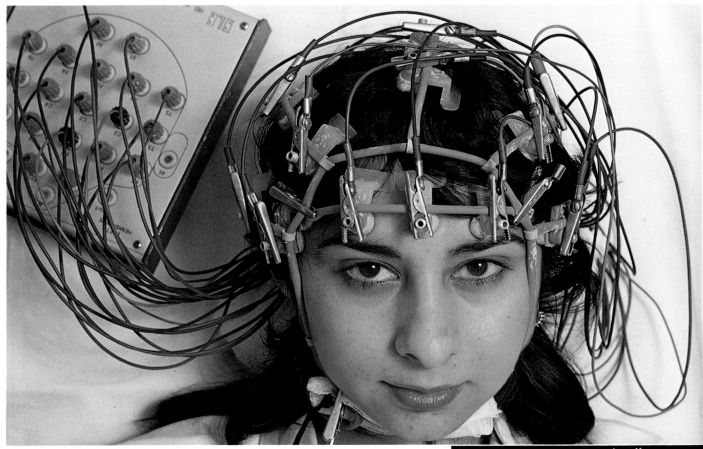

BEYOND THE BRAIN

MANY SCIENTISTS BELIEVE THAT THE MIND IS NOTHING BUT AN ASPECT OF THE ELECTRICAL AND CHEMICAL CHANGES THAT OCCUR IN THE BRAIN. IS THERE ANY EVIDENCE FOR THIS?

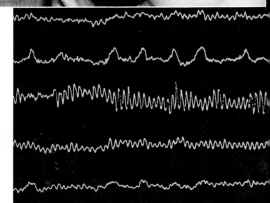

Our dreams, desires, memories, feelings and thoughts, our hopes and fears – even the way in which we experience the world around us – are nothing more than the product of chemical and electrical changes inside our brains. So when the brain stops functioning at the time of death, all mental activity ceases; and there is no possibility of our conscious survival of bodily death.

This, at any rate, is the belief that arises from the philosophy of materialism. According to this view, life arose purely by chance in a purposeless Universe, animals and plants evolved as the result of nothing more than chance genetic mutations and the blind forces of natural selection, and Man is

The subject, above, is wired up to an electroencephalograph machine (EEG), which monitors the electrical impulses produced by the brain. The typical EEG, above right, shows a read-out from a normal brain. EEG printouts present the characteristic patterns associated with different states of brain activity – waking, deep sleep, dreaming and so on – but cannot reveal the actual thoughts passing through the mind of the patient at the time.

nothing more than a complicated machine. But this is not a theory that can ever be proven; what is more, in many respects, it is an atheistic creed.

Nevertheless, materialists often speak as if the success of science in dealing with the physical and chemical aspects of life supports the idea that life is nothing but a complicated set of chemical and physical mechanisms. The fact is, however, that many aspects of life have eluded explanation in purely mechanistic terms. The way in which trees grow from seeds and animal embryos from fertilised eggs, for example, clearly involves far more than the production of the right kinds of chemicals.

Scientist Rupert Sheldrake has proposed an alternative theory to account for the inherited abilities of animals and plants. According to this hypothesis, the form and behaviour of an organism is shaped by so-called 'morphogenetic fields', which impose order and pattern on physical processes within living tissues, including the brain. These

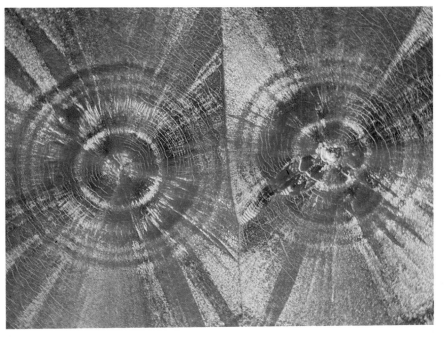

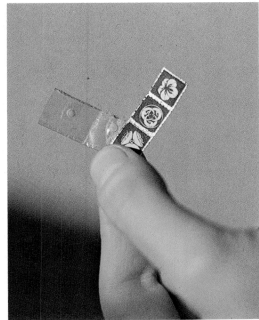

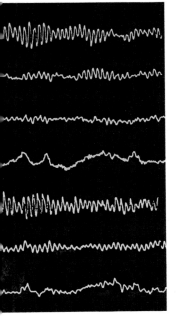

The photograph, top, is of hippuric acid, at a magnification of 150. The bright colours and abstract patterns are typical of certain types of drug-induced hallucination. Tiny amounts of lysergic acid diethylamide (LSD), for example, a colourless liquid that can be taken orally on small pieces of absorbent paper or bound with strychnine to form minute tablets or micro-dots, as shown top right, can produce hallucinations that go well beyond the normal range of activity of the human brain.

fields are built up by a process called 'morphic resonance' from past members of the species, and represent a kind of collective memory. Organisms 'tune in' to them, and through them, to both the form and the experiences of past members of their species. The genetic material, in the DNA of the genes, can affect the tuning system, but the shapes and instincts of the organism are not inherited *in* the DNA – just as people whose images appear on the screen of a television receiver are not carried *inside* the wires and transistors of the set. A correctly wired set is, of course, necessary for tuning in; but the factors that give rise to the pictures come from outside the set.

INFLUENCES FROM THE PAST

In a similar way, Sheldrake believes that the brain may be rather like a complicated tuning system. What is more, he believes, it is possible that it can be tuned to influences from its own past. This implies a theory of memory quite different from the conventional mechanistic theory, which assumes that all mental processes must depend on chemical or physical changes inside the brain. Perhaps memories are not, after all, stored as 'traces' in the nervous tissue, but are picked up by the brain as it tunes in to morphic resonance.

Materialists often argue that the fact that your state of mind can be influenced by physical and chemical changes in the brain shows that it is nothing but a product of brain activity. For example, consuming very small amounts of hallucinogenic drugs, such as LSD, can have dramatic subjective consequences. But this does not mean that conscious experience is nothing but an aspect of changes in the body. Take once again the analogy of a television set: the pictures on the screen can be affected by disturbing the wiring inside the set – or, for that matter, by pouring chemicals into it. But this does not mean that the pictures arise inside the set, or that the events shown on the screen are nothing but an aspect of what is happening within it. They do indeed depend on the set, but they also depend

on what the people are doing in the television studio, and on the electromagnetic waves by which the images are transmitted. If the set is badly damaged and the pictures on the screen disappear, the activity in the studio continues. In other words, the people whose pictures appeared on the screen have not been destroyed just because the set has 'gone dead'.

PATTERNS OF THE BRAIN

Measurements of electrical activity within the brain, using instruments such as the electroencephalograph (EEG), have shown that there are characteristic patterns associated with different states of consciousness – such as waking, deep sleep and dreaming. But while it is possible to tell from an EEG reading when someone is dreaming, for instance, we cannot identify what is actually going on in his or her dreams. It is rather like measuring the vibrations in a cinema projection room: they reveal whether the projector is projecting a film, rewinding, or switched off: but they cannot give any information about the subject matter of the film. Most of what is known about brain activity is as general as this. There is certainly no evidence that every image or thought that we experience is paralleled in detail by specific physical or chemical changes inside the brain.

Another analogy that can be used to help to demonstrate how states of mind depend on what happens in the brain, and vice versa, is provided by a pilot in an aeroplane. While the aeroplane is in flight, the pilot's actions are dictated by his interpretation of the readings on the many dials in the cockpit, wired up to instruments in various parts of the body of the aircraft. He also responds to what he sees in the sky around him and to radio messages from air traffic controllers on the ground. In turn, the actions of the pilot on the controls govern the thrust of the engine and the mechanisms that alter the direction and altitude of flight. But in spite of the fact that changes in the aeroplane influence the pilot, and changes in the pilot influence the aeroplane, the two are obviously not the same. When he has landed the aircraft, the pilot can get out and leave; and if the aeroplane is badly damaged in flight and seems likely to crash, the pilot will be able to bale out and parachute to safety.

In a similar way, the conscious self can control the body in the waking state, and is in turn influenced both by what happens within the body and in the environment around it, and also by what other people say. But in sleep and in dreams, your mind may not be so closely linked to the body.

Renewing the analogy, sleep and dreaming correspond to the state of the aeroplane on the ground, with its engine ticking over or switched off: under these conditions, the pilot can either leave the controls and wander around within the aeroplane, or leave it altogether. But even when the aeroplane is in flight, the pilot's state need not always be closely linked to the state of the aircraft: he can opt to put it under the control of the autopilot mechanism, and then chat with other members of the crew or read a book, say. Similarly, in the waking state, the mind may sometimes be less

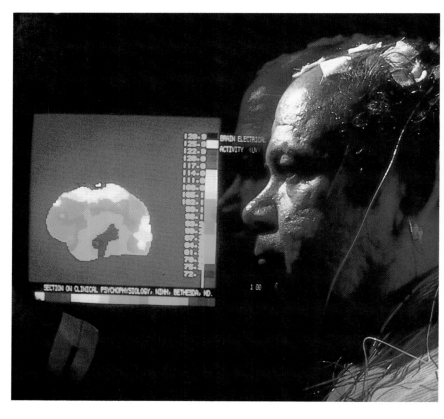

> **❚❚ THE CONSCIOUS SELF CAN BE THOUGHT OF AS INTERACTING NOT WITH A MACHINE, BUT WITH MOTOR FIELDS... IT 'ENTERS INTO' THE MOTOR FIELDS, BUT IT REMAINS OVER AND ABOVE THEM. ❚❚**
>
> **RUPERT SHELDRAKE,**
>
> **A NEW SCIENCE OF LIFE**

The photograph, above, shows a demonstration of mapping of the brain's activity in response to an electric shock to the right arm. The mind, according to the argument of materialists, is nothing but a product of brain activity.

The actions of a pilot and his craft, below left, are closely linked, but the man and the machine are clearly not the same thing.

closely connected with the state of the body than usual – when daydreaming or lost in thought, for instance.

One further analogy may also help to make the point that it is possible for the mind and the brain to be closely related without being one and the same thing. The brain may be compared with a complex computer. By itself, the computer 'hardware' can do nothing of significance. It is of use only when the right sort of programs are fed into it. These programs are not part of its wiring, but are created for particular purposes by a conscious,

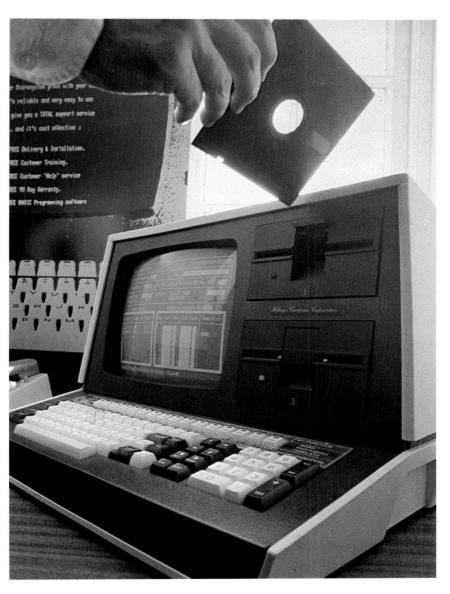

measured physically with scientific instruments. It eliminates the possibility of the existence of God and rejects all religious beliefs relating to life after death. But although this philosophy may have a certain intellectual appeal, does it in fact correspond to the way things really are? Or is it a gross over-simplification?

As to whether the mind and brain are identical, or that the mind is like a passive shadow of the brain, there is no evidence in favour of materialism that cannot be explained just as well, if not better, by the interactionist theory. There are even some very awkward facts that suggest the role of the brain may have been greatly overestimated in the past. It has, for instance, long been known that some people who have suffered from hydro-cephalus, or water on the brain, have greatly reduced amounts of brain tissue: the skull is mainly filled with fluid. In spite of this, they may be quite normal in their thought processes and behaviour.

DIMINISHED BRAINS
Studies on people of this type by Professor John Lorber, formerly of Sheffield University, using modern tissue-scanning techniques, have led him to ask, in a 1982 paper, *'Is Your Brain Really Necessary?'* He spoke of one case: 'There's a young student at this university who has an IQ of 126, has gained a first class degree in mathematics, and is socially completely normal. And yet the boy has virtually no brain.' The student's doctor at the university noticed that he had a slightly larger than normal head, and so referred him to Lorber, simply out of interest. 'When we did a brain scan on him,' Lorber continued, 'we saw that instead of the normal 4.5 centimetre [2-inch] thickness of brain tissue between the ventricles and the cortical surface, there was just a thin layer of mantle measuring a millimetre or so.'

Lorber's findings pose a dramatic challenge to conventional ideas about the role of the brain, and are a severe embarrassment to materialistic theories of the mind.

When it comes to the question of the possible personal survival of bodily death, the materialist theory again conflicts with other views – particularly the evidence from Spiritualist phenomena, memories of past lives in cases suggestive of reincarnation, and the apparent separability of the centre of consciousness from the body in out-of-the-body and near-death experiences. Even if some of this evidence can be explained in terms of telepathy, clair-voyance or precognition rather than in terms of the survival of the conscious self or soul, recognition of the existence of such parapsychological powers would mean that the mind has properties other than those explicable in terms of physics. Unfortunately, however, since all this evidence lies outside the scope of orthodox science, materialists can only ignore it or attempt to dismiss it.

There is, according to Sheldrake, no persuasive logical, philosophical or scientific reason why we should accept the materialist theory that the mind is nothing but an aspect of the functioning of the brain. The idea that the mind interacts with the body seems to make more sense of actual experience. What is more, it leaves open the possibility of a conscious survival of death.

intelligent person – the computer programmer. The programmer's activities, meanwhile, are influenced by the way the computer performs, and the computer is in turn influenced by the programs; but the programmer and the computer can in no way be considered one and the same.

The idea that the conscious self and the body interact with each other but not as aspects of the same thing is known as 'dualism' or 'interaction-ism'. It is the view taken by most of the greatest philosophers from Plato onwards. Indeed, an authoritative statement to this effect has been made in a book called *The Self and its Brain,* written jointly by Sir Karl Popper, a distinguished – and often controversial – philosopher of science, and Sir John Eccles, an eminent brain scientist. Meanwhile, the theory that the mind is nothing but an aspect of the functioning of the brain continues to be defended by materialist philosophers, the debate seemingly never-ending.

What, then, is the main attraction of material-ism? It seems to offer a relatively simple and straightforward view of the Universe in terms of matter and the laws of physics. It proclaims that there is only one kind of reality – that which can be

The mind and brain interact but are not synonymous. The operator, above, is shown feeding a floppy disk – which stores information – into a microcomputer. Materialists like to point out that the brain itself may be compared with a giant computer – but a computer is nothing without its program, which has to be created by an intelligent human being.

The Roman mosaic, left, shows the nine muses, daughters of Zeus and Mnemosyne, who were considered to govern all aspects of the arts. The origin of creative inspiration, for the ancient Greeks and Romans, was to be found with these goddesses – not inside the head.

THE HEALING TRANCE

In the 1850s, a man had a leg amputated while under hypnosis, but eminent doctors accused him of pretending to feel no pain. How much faith does modern medicine put in use of hypnotherapy?

The illustration, right, shows doctors in Munich, in 1893, tentatively exploring the hypnotic state. Almost a century later, Pierina Menegazzo, below, joked with the surgeon as he removed her appendix. She had been hypnotized to feel no pain but was still able to hold a conversation.

The story of hypnotherapy is one of the most disturbing, as well as one of the saddest, in the history of medicine. It has offered us what is potentially an immensely valuable therapeutic weapon that has never been properly exploited – and it is still generally neglected, in spite of the considerable evidence in its favour.

Hypnosis has a long history. There are indications, for instance, that a hypnotic element entered into ancient tribal medicine, and that it was used in the Aesculapian temples of healing in ancient Greece. But the first clear demonstration of its powers in modern times came as a result of experiments conducted by some of Franz Mesmer's disciples, two centuries ago. They found that they could relieve, and often remove, the symptoms of illness in mesmerized subjects. In particular, they could banish pain.

As there were no anaesthetics available at the time, this ought to have been a boon for patients undergoing surgery. Surgeons, however, would have none of it. When, in 1829, a Commission appointed by the French Academy of Medicine to investigate mesmerism watched an operation in which a tumour was painlessly removed, its members were impressed, but the medical establishment simply refused to accept that the case could have been genuine.

To Sir Benjamin Brodie, a fashionable London surgeon of the 1850s, mesmerism was nothing more than 'a debasing superstition'.

After watching a man having a leg amputated while in a mesmeric trance, the eminent physiologist Marshall Hall explained that the man must have

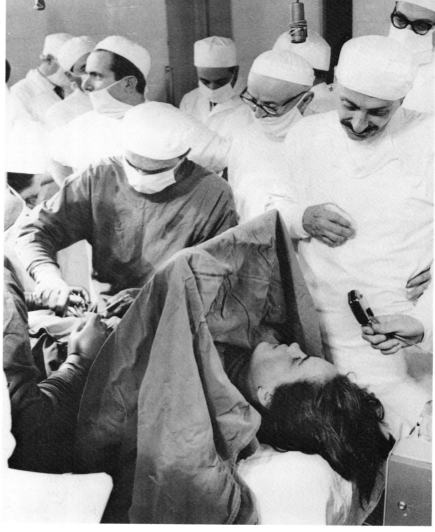

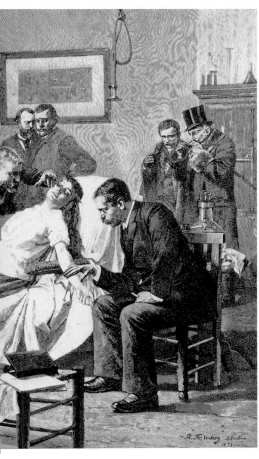

Considering what the alternatives were – bleeding, cupping, purging, and useless drugs – the patients must be considered to have been exceptionally lucky.

All this time, the medical establishment had refused to accept that hypnotism even existed, let alone that it could be used as a therapy; but in the 1880s, Jean-Martin Charcot managed to convince a committee of the Academy of Medicine that it was genuine – that people really could be put into a state of hypnotic trance. He did so, however, only by persuading them that the state of trance was linked with hysteria, so that it need not be taken seriously as a therapy. And in spite of Bernheim's continuing demonstrations that hypnotherapy was a simple and effective way of dealing with everyday disorders, doctors still shied away from it.

A committee appointed by the British Medical Association went to Nancy and returned in 1892 to report that Bernheim's methods worked. Hypnotherapy, they could confirm, would be an asset in Britain. Their verdict was ignored, however; and by the turn of the century, hypnotherapy had faded out of the picture. It was not repudiated, the French psychiatrist Pierre Janet was later to recall; it simply fell into disuse.

Hypnotherapy sessions, such as that below, are quite widely used today – by non medically-qualified practitioners – in the attempt to relieve such conditions as anxiety states, pre-examination nerves and addiction to nicotine or alcohol.

been only pretending not to feel pain; if he had really been unconscious, his other leg surely would have been seen to twitch in sympathy.

Anybody who has read contemporary accounts of what surgery was like in those days will appreciate just what it would have meant to thousands of agonized patients to have a mesmerist on hand. The coolies in the service of the East India Company in Calcutta were fortunate; they had James Esdaile as their surgeon. In the 1840s, he performed hundreds of operations while his patients were entranced. But the medical journals in England would not credit his accounts; and by that time, in any case, ether and chloroform were at last becoming available.

James Braid, who coined the term hypnotism to describe his method of inducing the mesmeric trance state, did not make much use of it as a therapy, but his work on it led a French country doctor, A. A. Liébeault, to try out hypnotherapy on patients in the late 1870s. If they wanted drugs, they could have them, he would say, but they would have to pay. Hypnotism would cost them nothing. Being thrifty (and poor), most opted for hypnotism.

So successful was Liébeault's form of treatment – having hypnotized the patients, he simply suggested to them that their symptoms would go away – that it attracted the attention of Hippolyte Bernheim, professor of medicine at the nearby town of Nancy. At first sceptical, he became a convert after a visit to Liébeault, in 1882; and for the first – and, as things turned out, last – time, hypnotherapy established itself as a routine form of hospital treatment.

Le Magnétisme.

Unquestionably, the main reason was that, in this period, the theory established itself that physical, 'organic' diseases could only be treated successfully by physical means – drugs or surgery. Hypnotherapy might be all right for people suffering from neuroses or hysteria, but not for people suffering from coughs and colds, let alone from more serious disorders. So, although a few individual doctors continued to use it, along with dentists who found it useful when patients reacted badly to 'jabs', little was heard of hypnotherapy for about half-a-century.

CONGENITAL CONDITION

The first reminder of just how unwise the British medical profession was to ignore hypnotherapy came in the *British Medical Journal* in 1952. This was a report on the case of a boy suffering from congenital ichthyosis – a condition that caused a warty layer, with a foul odour, to cover most of his body. After all the standard forms of treatment had failed, he had been taken to the hospital at East Grinstead in Surrey, where remarkable feats of plastic surgery had been achieved during the Second World War, to see if skin from parts of his body that were unaffected could be grafted to replace the affected areas; but that was equally ineffective.

One of the doctors at the hospital suggested that, as a last resort, they should try hypnotism. The boy was put into a trance and told that the condition of his left arm would clear. (They decided to proceed in this way so that if the warty layer disappeared only from his arm, it would be related to the suggestion, and could not be dismissed as coincidence). After a few days, the scaly layer on the arm softened, and fell off, showing that the skin underneath was normal in texture. And, in time, the condition later disappeared altogether.

Not merely was the 'rhino boy' – as press reports called him – healed, he was able to return to live the full social life that his appearance (and repulsive smell) had previously denied him. The report on his case concluded that although, formerly, he had been lonely and solitary, he had become, a year after the treatment, 'a happy, normal boy' and had also found a job.

It would be gratifying to be able to record that this case caused a change of heart in the medical establishment. But, in fact, it made very little perceptible difference. The fact is that most doctors had for so long been conditioned to assume that organic diseases can be treated only by organic methods that they could not think in any other terms. Even today, when the medical profession is widely aware that this dogma has been discredited, most doctors continue to diagnose disorders, and prescribe for them, as though it were still gospel.

A minority of doctors and dentists do use hypnotism; but the chief impetus behind what appears to be a current revival has come from practitioners who are not qualified members of the medical profession. Some of them have no qualifications at all; some have had training courses, often of doubtful value; and some are qualified psychologists who have decided to enter this territory.

What, then, is good hypnotherapy? There are many different answers to this question; but for

Dr A A Liébeault, (standing, above left, with some of his staff and patients at his clinic in Nancy, France, in 1900), was one of the most significant figures in the history of hypnotherapy.

> ❝ AS THE MIND GROWS, THE PROCESS OF DEVELOPMENT IS ENCUMBERED WITH PROCESSES OF BLOCKING, EVEN SUPPRESSING THIS POTENTIAL. HYPNOSIS ALLOWS THOSE NATURAL ABILITIES TO BE FREED. ❞
>
> **PROFESSOR DR ARTUR PETROVSKY, RUSSIAN PSYCHOLOGICAL SOCIETY**

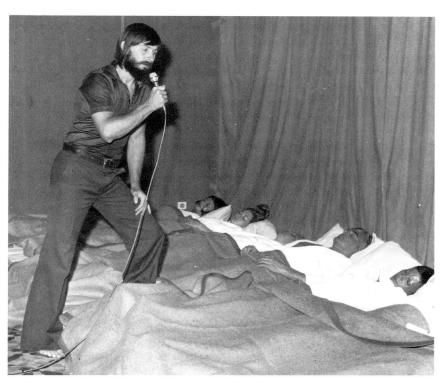

simplicity, hypnotherapy can be divided into two main categories. It can be used as Liébeault used it, simply as a means of getting rid of unwanted symptoms – in particular, pain. In this capacity, it is on a par with chemical analgesics such as aspirin; but, although rapport has to be established first between therapist and patient, which takes time (and not all patients are susceptible), there are no adverse side effects, and no prescription charges.

Most hypnotherapists, however, regard their work as being a branch of psychotherapy; and this means that they use hypnosis as an aid in whatever type of psychotherapy – Freudian, behaviourist or pragmatic – they favour. A plate on the door, or an entry in the classified telephone directory, saying simply 'Hypnotherapist' consequently affords no clue whatsoever to the kind of treatment patients – or 'clients', as many hypnotherapists refer to them – may expect.

SPEEDY ANALYSIS

Freud himself used hypnosis for a time, to regress his patients to the age at which their emotional conflicts had first been repressed, but he came to the conclusion that it did not disclose repressed material satisfactorily, and replaced it with the technique of free association that came to be known as psychoanalysis. Some of his disciples, however, decided that, for all its possible disadvantages, the use of hypnosis could enormously speed up the process of analysis. In the USA, particularly, it is now extensively used for this purpose.

Hypnotherapy might appear to have been just what the behaviourists needed, providing them with an easy way to implant ideas in patients' minds. But establishing the rapport with patients that is needed for successful hypnosis irked some behaviourists. Others were disappointed to find that the effects of suggestion soon wear off, like the effects of a drug. They were also, as Professor

The group, above, consented to take part in an extremely effective cure for insomnia, and were plunged into a hypnotically-induced sleep by Jacquy Nuguet for a record 10 days in Nice, France. At intervals, they were partly roused to sip orange juice and have their other needs attended to. The 'operation' was conducted under medical supervision.

Using only a torch and hypnosis, Alan Paige, below, has total control over three circus elephants.

Hans Eysenck observed in *Sense and Nonsense in Psychology,* put off by the 'unfortunate associations which the term hypnosis arouses in so many people' – associations with occultism, quackery, and music hall performance.

However, hypnotherapy is gradually shedding this image. A great deal of research is now being undertaken, most of it in the USA. Indeed, the survey in *Hypnosis at its Bicentennial,* edited by Fred H. Frankel of the Harvard Medical School, describes interesting results from trials of hypnosis in the treatment of, among other conditions, burns, migraine, asthma and impotence. Enormous progress has also been made in the exploitation of hypnotic regression. Freud rejected this himself, possibly because he was not very good at it. Distancing himself from his patients, in the name of scientific objectivity, he deprived himself of the ability to collaborate with them, as it were, on the last stretch of their journey back in time. Indeed, it seems that just when they needed a metaphorical (and perhaps actual) hand to hold, he was keeping out of reach, and out of sight, behind the couch.

Paradoxically, the fact that recall and subsequent release of long repressed emotions under hypnotic regression will often suffice to remove or relieve a variety of disorders is now helping towards an understanding between the Freudian and the behaviourist schools. It used to be, and to some extent still is, axiomatic among behaviourists that there is no need to go burrowing back into the past. Neurotic symptoms are, according to strict behaviourist beliefs, no more than an indication of learned behaviour, which simply needs to be unlearned. But with hypnotic regression, the process of finding the repressed emotional conflict, inspecting it and then releasing the tension has been found to have such an immediate and striking an effect on symptoms that this old preconception is being broken down.

Hypnotherapists today totally reject the Svengali image. Their aim, rather, is use of hypnosis to reveal to the patient what his own mind is capable of accomplishing – for hypnotic suggestion, however effective in the short term, is not lasting. For maximum results, the patient must learn how to play his own part in his therapy.

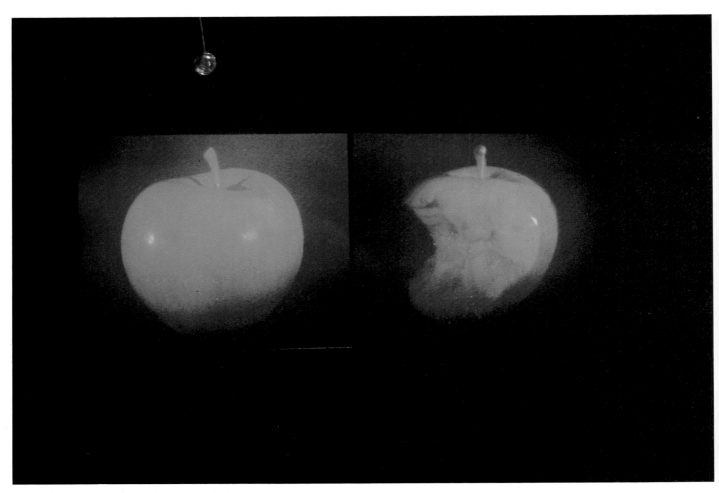

BETRAYED BY THE SENSES

CONCEPTIONS OF REALITY VARY CONSIDERABLY AMONG INDIVIDUALS. THE QUESTION INEVITABLY REMAINS, THEREFORE, AS TO WHO PERCEIVES WITH ACCURACY

In psychiatric literature, there are numerous examples of quite well people who have, for a period, experienced hallucinations that they knew to be illusory yet behaved as if the experiences were genuine. These viewers seemed able to walk right around their hallucinations, which were apparently real enough to them to block out light and objects, to be reflected in mirrors and even appear in double images when the sides of

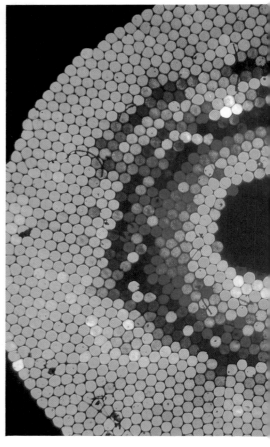

Our perception of the world is not always what it seems. The hologram of an apple, above, for instance, looks 'real' enough, yet it is only an image created by lasers. Some animals, meanwhile, see the world quite differently from the way we do. A bee might see the eye of a bird as huge and segmented, right. Dolphins, far right, however, use sonar with which to 'see' – and even, it is believed, possess a form of X-ray vision.

the viewers' eyeballs were pressed, just as real objects do. But since these images had no objective reality, there was no way in which light could possibly travel from the hallucinations and affect the eyes so as to register an image in the brain.

Yet, in such cases, the image is definitely there – for at least one person. This must mean that, instead of light travelling from a real object, registering on and being interpreted by the viewer's brain, the brain itself must create an image and in some way 'project' it to the spot where it is seen. Similar processes must also occur in hallucinations affecting the other senses – hearing, for instance.

There are, certainly, many types of hallucination that occur when the subject is awake, sleeping, in a trance, under hypnosis or only semi-awake.

PERCHANCE TO DREAM

Everyone, to be sure, experiences the hallucinations of dreams. Much of what we dream consists of unimportant fragments of memory, dramatisations of anxieties or desires escaping from subconscious repression, or sometimes simply the communication of physical discomfort – such as a dream of being suffocated when a pillow has slipped across one's face. Some extraordinary dreams, with startling vividness and impact on the dreamer, may also be significantly precognitive. These are, in many ways, picture-shows inside the dreamer's mind and correspond to no external reality that his or anyone else's physical senses can appreciate at the time. Yet, if they do prove precognitive, they are the shadows of coming events, and as real as the shadow of a man overtaking you when the evening sun is at your back.

Queen Mary I (1516-1558), whose marriage to Philip II of Spain resulted in a phantom pregnancy, is seen, right, in a detail from a painting on wood by Sir Anthony Moore that is exhibited in The Prado, Madrid. In such cases, all outward appearances indicate the progress of pregnancy: the woman ceases to menstruate and may suffer from morning sickness and other allied conditions – but there is no baby. It seems that it is the intense desire of the frustrated mother that creates the cruel illusion of motherhood.

MANY CASES HAVE BEEN REPORTED WHERE A FIGURE OR AN OBJECT IN A DREAM HAS BEEN PROLONGED INTO A VIVID WAKING HALLUCINATION.

D.H. RAWCLIFFE, OCCULT AND SUPERNATURAL PHENOMENA

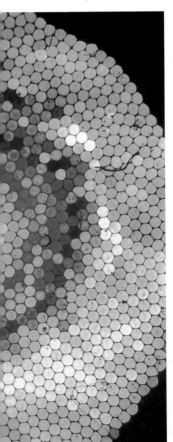

A TRICK OF THE MIND?

Some years ago, author David Christie-Murray was invited to lecture on psychical research at a school. He was given dinner before the talk by the housemaster who had arranged the lecture. Another guest was the mother of two boys at the school, who told Christie-Murray the following story.

The woman had always longed for a daughter and, when her two sons were in their teens, she adopted a baby girl whom she came to adore. But, sadly, when the girl was still only a toddler, she was killed in a car crash. What was worse, the woman said, she herself had been driving the car at the time, and the accident had been entirely her fault. The loss of the child and the sense of crushing guilt made life doubly agonising for the grieving mother.

One night, some time after the tragedy, she suddenly woke up and, overwhelmed by sorrow and feeling the need of comfort and companionship, tried to wake her husband. But it was impossible: he seemed to be in some kind of coma. In the end, she gave up and, in utter desolation, went into what had been the child's bedroom and sat on her bed.

Quite suddenly, she realised that the little girl was standing in front of her. She held out her hands and said 'Mummy'. The mother spontaneously opened her arms to the child, who climbed on to her lap and laid her head on her shoulder. It seemed miraculous: her daughter had died but here she was, solid and warm, flesh and blood – a 'living' child whose hair could be felt against the breast. They sat in their joyful embrace for a short time. Then the little girl clambered down from her mother's lap, said 'Mummy, I have to go now,' and promptly vanished just as mysteriously as she had appeared.

The experience left the mother with a great sense of joy – an emotion as intense, in fact, as her previous desolation – and a total conviction of the survival of bodily death and some sort of after-life.

David Christie-Murray said of this quite extraordinary experience: 'There was no doubt about the emotion and sincerity with which she told her story and, if she was a pretender trying to hoodwink a psychical researcher of long standing, she was a very convincing actress. If the experience was genuine, as I do not doubt it was, at least it shows that not all "otherworldly" encounters are hostile, sinister or sick.'

This story seems to confirm the Spiritualist belief that departed souls can materialise in some sort of solid form. But others may well dismiss such an experience as a mere trick of the mind – the nature of this, in itself, being very much a mystery.

CASEBOOK

or perhaps even visitations from another dimension. Some of the images experienced at these times seem so overwhelmingly vivid that even the most hardened sceptic experiencing them finds it impossible to believe that they do not correspond to some reality.

Cultural expectations, researchers have found, often dictate the content of such hallucinations. Indeed, in ages of greater superstition – or faith – assisted by drugs, fasting, mortification of the flesh and meditation, individuals have often experienced either the orgies of the witches' sabbats, or visions and communications from angels, the Virgin and Christ. In our age, a similar kind of cultural conditioning may also explain the experience of the woman who, while seated beside her friends in a car, gave a running commentary that described how she was being taken on board a UFO.

This experience is in many respects akin to the hallucinations of hypnosis, in which especially receptive subjects can be made to see people and

In medieval times, there was great fear of incubi and succubi – respectively male and female demons who would have sex with sleeping women and men. They were often blamed for the sexual dreams that people had from time to time. But modern psychiatry has in fact discovered that some somnambules (sleep-walkers) can have such vivid sexual fantasies in dreams that they reach orgasm. A further remarkable hallucination is that of the phantom pregnancy: one famous historical example is that of Mary I of England (who ruled from 1553-58). She so yearned for a child that, for a full nine months, she showed all the signs of imminent motherhood.

Even more astonishing are reported accounts of spectral rape. A significant number of women have reported this experience, both while sleeping and while awake – developing, during the ghostly assault, all manner of bruises, scratches and bites that could not possibly have been self-inflicted, even as a result of the hysteria induced by sexual repression and guilt – the usual medical explanation for such experiences. There are even instances where members of the victim's family claim to have seen a ghostly attacker dissolving before their eyes.

STIGMATA OF THE MIND

In spectral rape, it is most likely, however, that the explanation is a psychological one. Other related phenomena, too, seem to originate in the mind. A knife-slash, for instance, has been known to appear on the face of a man reliving a brawl under the influence of drugs or hypnosis. A girl, believing herself to be the reincarnation of a slave flogged to extinction, collapsed on what she thought was the place of her death, whiplashes appearing spontaneously across her back. Such wounds are patently not self-inflicted physically, yet may be brought about mentally. As for the shadowy rapist seen by others, he could be, of course, an hysteric vision, created and then communicated by the victim to others.

Some of these phenomena are experienced while falling asleep (when they are termed hypnagogic), and some during the process of waking. These are the two twilight times in everyone's day, when we are all particularly open to hallucinations

It is said that what mystics see and feel while in their ecstasies is so different from everyday reality that there are no words to describe their experiences. The fourth-century St Anthony, having cut himself off from the world, was constantly beset by demons, as shown, above, in a painting by Bosch. He believed them to be 'real' enough to see and communicate with but, drawing on his faith, he could also dismiss them at will. A more modern mystic was the 19th-century writer Emily Brontë, right, whose ecstatic trances contrasted sharply with her everyday world of baking bread and supervision of her Yorkshire household.

objects that are not actually there, and not to see others that are. So how 'real' is the mustard that is tasted by both subject and hypnotist – although only the hypnotist has put it in his mouth? Or the pinprick or pinch felt by the subject but inflicted on the hypnotist?

Evidence points to the existence of many kinds of reality. One that is quite different from our workaday world, for instance, is that of the mystic or visionary who, when in an altered state of consciousness, suddenly becomes at one with the whole of the Universe and its source. He or she may even remember this moment of insight with a clarity that makes day-to-day reality seem as nebulous and insignificant as a dream. But whether other levels of reality are halfway houses between the commonplace world and the mystics' ultimate reality, or whether some manifestations of them – such as hallucinations – are merely the aberrations of disturbed minds is a matter that, for the present, remains to be determined.

ENCOUNTERS OF THE MIND

HYPNOTIZED SUBJECTS TAKING PART IN AN EXPERIMENT GAVE IMAGINARY ACCOUNTS OF UFO ENCOUNTERS THAT WERE REMARKABLY LIKE 'REAL' REPORTS. COULD IT BE THAT ALIEN – AND SUPERNATURAL – ENTITIES ARE ALL IN THE MIND?

In March 1971, Brian Scott and a friend (who wishes to be known by the pseudonym of Eric Wilson) were camping in the Arizona desert. One evening, at around 9 p.m., they saw a brilliant object hovering in the sky, some 5 miles (8 kilometres) away. It was oval-shaped and dark, but there was a bright haze around it and a brilliant purple light beneath it. Scott pointed his flashlight at it, whereupon it began to approach them. When the object was overhead, it was so huge that it almost blocked out the sky, hovering over them at a height

of some 200 feet (60 metres) and bathing them in purple light. They could see no windows, doors or other features of conventional aircraft.

Scott remembered nothing more until they were in the car and travelling homewards, when a time signal on his car radio revealed that it was 11 p.m. Two hours had elapsed, which neither of them could recall.

Some four years later, when Scott was 32 years old, he told a colleague of the experience and followed up the suggestion that he should report it to UFO researchers. Their investigation led to a hypnosis session, in the hope that it would help him to recall additional details.

The anima mundi *– 'soul of the world' – right, is from an 18th-century manuscript. Such representations conform to Jung's theory of archetypes which says that certain symbolic images, lying in the unconscious, have universal significance. Jung himself argued that UFOs and UFO entities are archetypal symbols.*

The illustration, **left,** *is from Bertrand Meheust's book of 1978, in which he argued that there were remarkable similarities between UFO accounts of the 1970s and science fiction stories of earlier periods. In most cases, however, those who reported the UFO sightings could not have read the stories – nor even have heard of them.*

*In*Focus

SLEEPING WITH THE DEVIL

In a home near Moray Firth in Scotland, a young virgin was seduced by a 'marvellous beautiful youth', and confessed to her parents that she did not know where he came from nor where he went after their love-making. However, when the girl's parents broke into her bedroom, they found not a handsome youth but a hideous monster. The girl's lover was an incubus – a devil who forces sex on women. (A lustful devil who seduces men – as *above* – is known as a succubus.)

The story comes from a 17th-century compilation of 'operations of witches against the human race', collected by a monk from an obscure order in Milan, Italy. He says at the start: 'Almost all the Theologians and learned Philosophers are agreed, and it has been the experience of all times and all nations, that witches practise coition with demons, the men with Succubus devils and the women with Incubus devils.'

Such sexual intercourse, for which even pleading rape was no defence, was punishable by the Church. During the witch-hunts of the 16th and 17th centuries, this could mean horrible torture, often ending in death.

Medieval demonologists maintained that incubi and succubi could assume human form, either as apparitions or in the flesh, by using a dead body. Indeed, it was common for the demons to take on the form of the husband, wife or lover of the person they seduced. Deceived in this way or not, the mortal was guilty of committing a great sin in the eyes of the Church. Being assaulted by an incubus or succubus, however, was very different from possession, for the possessed was regarded as a victim and was given help through exorcism. But it was believed that the sex devils could withstand exorcism. So, paradoxically, anybody trafficking with them had to take the blame and bear the full punishment.

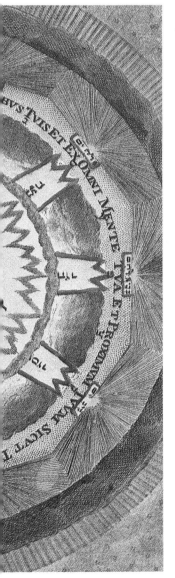

Under hypnosis, Scott said that he and Wilson had been taken into the UFO, where tall and ugly entities, with three-fingered hands, had forced them to submit to a physical examination. The alien leader had been distant but not unfriendly. He said he came from 'another world, beyond all time, through years of light years... ' He told Scott: 'When I return, all will know the truth. Life will be lived through all time and knowledge will all be yours... I am now, I was, and always will be.' In addition to these somewhat vague statements, Scott reported more specific predictions as to Earth's future, including 'the complete annihilation of the Western hemisphere' from an easterly direction and involving bombs of high magnitude. But a few thousand persons were to be saved and taken to another plane of existence, on 24 December 2011.

Wilson did not corroborate Scott's account. In fact, he was reluctant even to admit that they had sighted a UFO, let alone that they had been abducted. Asked if he thought it possible that Scott had invented the whole affair, he said it was.

Eventually, Wilson did allow himself to be hypnotized, but it did not affect his story. The hypnotist then suggested that he should forget about what *did* happen, and describe instead what he thought *might* have happened, if a UFO sighting had actually taken place. 'I want you to use your imagination now. I want you to pretend you can see these things.' Wilson then gave an account. But was it fact or fiction? The investigator, John DeHerrerra, afterwards speculated:

'With this nagging doubt about the validity of the information obtained from a hypnotized witness, I thought it would be wise to conduct an experiment. If someone, under hypnosis, could be encouraged to visualize and describe an imaginary UFO abduction, how would it compare with a supposedly "real" case? I shared this idea with the professor [Alvin Lawson] and the physician [Dr W. C. McCall]. They thought it was a great idea, so we began making preparations.'

The experiment that followed, starting in early 1977, was arguably one of the most significant in the history of research into the paranormal. Indeed, its findings require us to take a fresh look at the interpretation of sighting reports.

Subjects for the experiment were recruited by means of an advertisement in a college newspaper, and were screened to eliminate anyone with a particular knowledge of or interest in UFOs. Like Wilson, they were asked, under hypnosis, to imagine themselves in a UFO encounter, and were encouraged by leading – but non-specific – questions to provide a detailed account. The results were astonishing, for the imaginative accounts were found to be strikingly similar to the reports of allegedly 'real' abductees, with which the subjects could not have been familiar.

The experimenters wondered if the hypnotized subjects were somehow tuning in to the hypnotist, picking up his knowledge of UFO accounts and 'playing it back' as a personal experience. But even granting telepathy and the known tendency for hypnotized subjects to tell the hypnotist what he wants to hear, it may be considered to be stretching things to suggest that every subject taking part in the experiment was telepathic. It seemed more likely that some other process was at work.

Whatever that process may turn out to be, the DeHerrerra-Lawson-McCall experiment indicates that it is possible for people to imagine an experience in such detail that they seem somehow to have had access to information that was theoretically beyond their reach.

Many people concluded that these results invalidated *all* abduction reports: it seemed reasonable to suppose that the allegedly 'real' abductees could easily have invented their experiences, just as the volunteer subjects had done. But Lawson insisted that this was not a necessary consequence of the experiment. He pointed to conspicuous differences between the fictitious and the real accounts, not so much in *what* was said as in *how* it was conveyed.

UFOs and Science Fiction

But there are other findings that are relevant to the question. In 1978, in his book *Science Fiction et Soucoupes Volantes (Science Fiction and Flying Saucers)*, the French ufologist Bertrand Meheust discussed the extraordinary similarities between accounts of UFO sightings in the 1970s and science fiction stories written half-a-century earlier – similarities that might have been ascribed to coincidence if they had occurred only once or twice, but not when they happened as often as Meheust found.

How can we account, for instance, for the fact that, in 1976, an illiterate farmer in Argentina described an experience that matches in detail a story written for a French pulp science fiction magazine of the 1920s?

In 1977, another Frenchman, Michel Monnerie, drew attention to the significance of certain *identified* flying object reports; while in *The UFO Handbook,* the American ufologist Allan Hendry also emphasized the value of studying such cases. In one instance that Hendry cited, an intelligent middle-aged woman described how she had seen a cigar-shaped UFO with windows, through which she could see the shapes of silver-suited occupants; but investigators proved beyond doubt that what she had in fact seen was the planet Venus.

There is nothing new about mistaking Venus for a UFO. But why should it be that witnesses, seemingly in all sincerity, so frequently add completely fictitious details to their descriptions of what has been seen?

The planet Venus, right, has often been mistaken for a UFO. In such instances, witnesses usually add details such as windows and occupants.

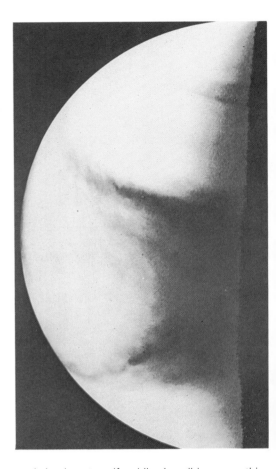

It is almost as if, while describing something they have not seen, witnesses somehow obtain the necessary details to fabricate their account. Could there be some kind of 'image bank' from which their unconscious minds borrow information?

Such a hypothesis brings us close to Carl Gustav Jung's concept of the 'collective unconscious', a sort of reservoir of ideas and symbols that all of us share, and that we can draw on in the form of archetypes – symbolic forms that have broadly the same significance for us all. But the 'image bank' concept goes further, for it involves specific details that hardly qualify as universal symbols, but that occur time and time again in the eyewitness reports. A UFO might be seen as an archetype, but the addition of a row of windows with silver-suited aliens peering out from them is an elaboration that surely takes it quite some way beyond the 'collective unconscious' theory.

It may well be that the reason why some people see one thing and some another is related to the personal and cultural background of the witness. Visions of the Virgin Mary are seen mostly by Catholics, rarely by Protestants, and almost never by non-Christians, for example. This may be accounted for by arguing that the Virgin chooses to manifest only to those who have faith in her, but it is equally well explained by suggesting that visions must be relevant to the beliefs and values of those who see them. Country people, in the medieval period, deprived and repressed, had visions of being abducted by fairies to take part in non-stop orgies of feasting and drinking. A modern schoolgirl, subconsciously seeking comfort or companionship, may be visited by a spacewoman who appears in

Michel Monnerie, below, the French author, suggested that the way in which people misconstrue identified flying objects is, in itself, highly significant and needs further study.

her bedroom and discusses her personal problems. Cases like these encourage the view that all such alleged experiences are purely psychological. It is in many ways the most plausible approach, and does not involve any 'supernatural' factors.

TRIGGER PROCESSES

If we think of entity sightings as originating within the witness, what is the process involved? It could perhaps be triggered by some need on the part of the witness, such as a sudden crisis; it could result from the wish of a subject to comply with the suggestions of a hypnotist; or it could just be a highly elaborated account of a sighting of something strange and inexplicable. If this is so, we must suppose that the unconscious mind of the witness fabricates a coherent incident, in terms suitable to individual circumstances, and that this is presented to the conscious mind as if it were a real event occurring in the external world.

But some such factor as the 'image bank' is required if we are to account for those cases in which witnesses display knowledge of matters beyond their experience. If the unconscious mind is indeed responsible, then it must have the ability to bring in images and ideas from external sources to assist in imagining the 'false' sighting.

This is an assumption that many may feel disinclined to make: but the only alternative is to assume that the sighting does originate externally. Then again, external origination is not necessarily discounted by the fact that a sighting is closely related to the individual's needs, hopes, fears or expectations. The Theosophical model accounts for this quite neatly. It assumes the existence of amorphous elementals, endowed with a great capacity for empathy. On the basis of the information they obtain from the mind of the witness, they instantaneously take on an appropriate form – one

The medieval woodcut, right, shows the fairy Melusine, as she leaves her mortal husband. She comes close in appearance to the strange creature reported by three American soldiers in Vietnam in 1969.

that will comfort, or frighten, or perhaps simply tease the witness – a benevolent alien visitor, a malevolent demon, or a dancing fairy, perhaps.

While on night duty in Vietnam in 1969, three American servicemen reported seeing an amazing flying creature – a naked black woman with wings. It seems unlikely that all three, even in the nervous state caused by night duty, would either imagine the same creature or misjudge a night-bird. But all three agreed as to its colour and shape, and knew they had seen something remarkable. Collective hallucination is sometimes offered as an explanation in such instances.

In this case, however, there does seem every reason to believe in the external reality of the entity; but at the same time, the fact has to be faced that, although winged humanoids have been reported on many occasions from different parts of the world, no such being is known to science. Indeed, the creature that most resembles the description given by the servicemen is the fairy Melusine, as depicted in medieval woodcuts.

Perhaps such entities face us with the challenge of a different kind of reality, a hitherto unexplored realm in which our current notions of what is real are no longer valid.

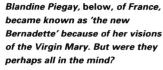

Blandine Piegay, below, of France, became known as 'the new Bernadette' because of her visions of the Virgin Mary. But were they perhaps all in the mind?

> **THE EXPERIMENTS ... DO SUGGEST THAT ANYONE WHO SUBCONSCIOUSLY WISHES TO DO SO [MAKE UP A STORY] IS ABLE TO FIND WITHIN HIMSELF THE NECESSARY RESOURCES.**
>
> **HILARY EVANS,**
> **GODS, SPIRITS, COSMIC GUARDIANS**

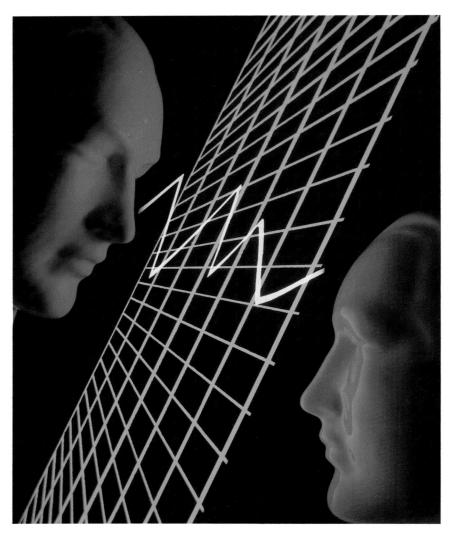

WAKING UP TO PSI

WHEN TWO PEOPLE COMPARE THEIR DREAMS, THEY MAY WELL UNCOVER TELEPATHIC LINKS. HERE, ESP RESEARCHER JOE FRIEDMAN TELLS OF HIS EXPERIMENTS IN THIS AREA

There are few examples of a sustained telepathic link between two people. One is the telepathic link between the American novelist Upton Sinclair and his wife Mary, a link that was tested in a series of ESP drawing experiments, subsequently described in detail in Sinclair's book *Mental Radio*. This book, published in 1930, so impressed Albert Einstein that he wrote an introduction to it.

The illustration, above, depicts the intriguing telepathic link that researchers have found in the dreams of certain subjects with a close relationship.

In the late 1970s, I myself was involved in a sustained and well-documented series of dreams that were telepathically linked to those of a close friend and former student of mine. Most of these dreams took place between May and December 1979. There were more than 20 in all, equally distributed between the two partners.

DREAM AWARENESS

Dave Ashworth first became a student in one of my parapsychology courses, held in London, in April 1978. Aged 23, he had been interested in the occult and psychical research for some time. He was also deeply aware of his dream life, often remembering and recording several dreams a night. After a class that I held on telepathic and precognitive dreams, Dave came up to me and said that, though he had been writing down his dreams for some time, he had never had one that he considered to be precognitive. I told him confidently that he would have such a dream the following week. In saying this, I was partly trying to bring about the desired result – but I also felt a genuine conviction that Dave would indeed have a precognitive dream.

The following week, however, he told me of the failure of his attempt. He had remembered and recorded 13 dreams during the week, but none of them had proved precognitive. I asked him to tell me just one. After looking through his dream diary, he recounted one in which, he said: 'The brat next door comes into my room. I am very hospitable and feed him, but he acts boorishly, as if he owns the place. He opens the wardrobe and, to my amazement, there is another door in the back of the wardrobe, which leads into the attic next door...'

I then told Dave he had just had his first telepathic dream. I had been intending to lead my class in a guided fantasy that evening: they would be urged to have a dream in which they opened their wardrobe door to find that there was another door in the back, a door that opened magically for them.

This experience inaugurated a telepathic dream series that was to last over two years and that was marked by an all-important factor – that of selection. In this case, Dave chose the psychic dream from a total of 13 that he had recorded during the week. He could hardly have picked out the 'right' dream by pure chance; so he must have had some awareness that this dream was precisely the psychic one for which he was looking. Later in the series, this awareness became more explicit, so that each of us became better able to pick out his own psychic dreams.

In March 1979, Dave joined a dream group that I was leading. We met fairly regularly, often once a week, for a period of a little more than a year. It was during this period that most of the psychic dreams occurred. We started the practice of telling each other any dreams in which the other figured. A high percentage contained correspondences with the dreams or waking life of the other person.

Often, Dave and I would dream of similar topics, themes or metaphors on the same night. In one such spontaneous coincidence, I dreamed of visiting a friend who lived in Colliers Wood in south London. In part of Dave's dream of that night, most of which involved eating at my flat, he dreamed of a picnic in a forest. As he recounted: 'All around are

Many psychoanalysts who have studied psychic dreams have encountered this sort of 'tracer' – an indication in the dream itself that it will prove psychic. Indeed, I have found that most people who have regular telepathic dreams have some sort of tracer in them. Psychic dreams also often have a peculiar quality of vividness. On other occasions, they might have a distinctive 'feel' to them. In Dave's psychic dreams, a grey cat often appeared. In other people's dreams, the tracer is to be found in the fact that the dream is set in a certain place of power.

SLEEPING DIALOGUE

Many of the dreams in our telepathic series contained such tracer elements. Their presence indicated that both of us were becoming more aware of the dream dialogue that was gradually developing between us.

people in orange clothes... some single, some in groups. They are either walkers or miners... There are stones and stone circles . . . I stand in one circle and am aware that this is a place of power. I touch my forehead to a tree and then wonder if I am emitting psychic power.'

Could those in the forest, possibly miners, be a reference to *Colliers* Wood? Whether or not this is so, the dream is important for other reasons. In it, Dave seems to have had an awareness that it was connected with me – he dreamt of eating a meal at my flat – and that the dream was psychic – he dreamt that he might be emitting psychic power.

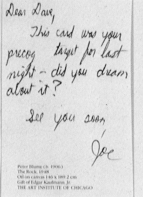

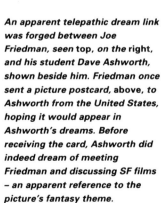

An apparent telepathic dream link was forged between Joe Friedman, seen top, on the right, and his student Dave Ashworth, shown beside him. Friedman once sent a picture postcard, above, to Ashworth from the United States, hoping it would appear in Ashworth's dreams. Before receiving the card, Ashworth did indeed dream of meeting Friedman and discussing SF films – an apparent reference to the picture's fantasy theme.

To test his wife's telepathic powers, American writer Upton Sinclair sent her the sketch of a bird's nest, above left, sealed in an envelope. After concentrating on the 'target', she made her own sketch of it, left. It closely resembles her husband's. Yet she did not see it as a bird's nest. Instead, she wrote on it: 'Inside of a rock well with vines climbing on outside.'

Another sort of psychic dream may involve a reference to an event occurring in the waking life of the other person in the friendship. In one such dream, I had gone to a park with a friend of Dave's and mine called Laura. According to my dream diary, while I was preoccupied with listening to some music that was being played in the park:

'A black youth started to remove my bike. I rushed over to him and started pushing him around, really enjoying myself, saying "What are you doing with my bike?" While I was doing this, the boy's father came and got on my bike and started to ride it off. I realised that I had allowed myself to get carried away... '

Shortly before I dreamed this, in the evening, I later learned that Dave had left his bike outside a friend's house during a visit. While he was inside, his rear light was stolen, for the second time from this location. On the way home, Dave fell to daydreaming of leaving his bike outside this house and hiding, waiting for the thief to come. He then caught the thief and gave him a good beating. His daydream continued with the boy's father coming to his friend's house and asking for the person who owned a bicycle.

I did several forms of informal experiment with Dave. In one, I bought a postcard that I thought would be a good target and sent it to him while I was on holiday in the United States. I wrote on the back: 'Dear Dave, This card was your precog. target

for last night – did you dream about it?'
In fact, Dave's dream on the night before he received the card did have a resemblance to the target. It was as follows:

'At Joe's, seeing him for the first time after the break. He tells me of some sci-fi film – did I see it? I didn't, but it seems Roy [Joe's flatmate] did. They talk about it. Joe then mentions a series of sci-fi fantasy films, but I have seen none of them.'

This science fiction or fantasy theme did seem to correspond with the picture on the postcard, which was a fantasy scene. Interestingly, I did not know the date of the postcard's arrival in England,

" SLEEP SEEMS TO BE ESPECIALLY SUITABLE FOR THE RECEPTION OF TELEPATHIC COMMUNICATION. **"**

SIGMUND FREUD,

DREAMS AND THE OCCULT

PERSPECTIVES

DEAR DIARY

If you wish to look for ESP in your dreams, it will be necessary to remember as many as you can, in as much detail as possible. Keep a notebook and pencil at your bedside and write down your dreams immediately you wake up. Often there may be only one fading image: but if you keep going over it in your mind, other parts of the dream will probably be recalled. If you can remember nothing of the dream, go over the thoughts you had at the moment of waking – these are likely to lead back to the dream. It is helpful to carry a notebook during the day to jot down remembered dream scenes that sometimes come to mind without warning.

Write down the dreams – in as much detail as you reasonably can. Selection will be necessary, however, so pay attention to any unusual detail that would provide strong evidence of the paranormal if it were also to occur in someone else's dream (or, indeed, in waking life).

Your partners in the experiment will, of course, need to keep equally detailed dream diaries. Resemblances between your dreams and theirs will undoubtedly occur: your problem will be to decide in an objective way which ones could not be due to coincidence.

and Dave did not even know of the experiment, since I had conceived of it on the spur of the moment. In the dream, there is also a clear tracer element: Dave dreams of seeing me for the first time since the holidays. The dream, seemingly, was a psychic 'meeting'. In the dream, I kept insisting that Dave must have seen one of the films I was telling him about, but he denied it. The dream itself seems to have been alluding to the postcard scene by not actually succeeding in showing it to the dreamer.

On another occasion, Dave picked up a photograph I was 'transmitting' to another group with which I was involved. On the night of this transmission, of which he had no knowledge, Dave dreamed:

'In a street I come unexpectedly upon Jeff [a friend] – he looks absolutely amazing, dressed in a yellow safari suit . . . with a butterfly net in one hand, stalking butterflies... There are many brightly coloured butterflies, large furry ones, yellow ones and somewhere amidst them all is one which is very special.'

The photograph showed a dance troupe which included a number of people wearing wings – they did indeed look like butterflies.

These are a few personal, well authenticated examples of dream telepathy. They suggest that two, or more, people who are open to the possibility of the paranormal can radically increase the amount and quality of ESP occurring in their lives by making a practice of remembering, recording and sharing their dreams.

The picture of a Chinese film set, below, was used as a target in one of the author's telepathy experiments. He 'sent' it to a group with which he was working. Dave Ashworth, who knew nothing of the experiment, dreamed that night of large, brightly coloured butterflies, and the actors in the background do, indeed, look rather like huge butterflies, because of their extravagant costumes.

HUMAN SALAMANDERS

FEAR OF FIRE IS DEEPLY ROOTED IN THE HUMAN PSYCHE — BUT SOME RARE PEOPLE SEEM TOTALLY IMMUNE TO HEAT AND FLAMES

The belief that the blacksmith is 'Master of Fire' is common in both ancient cultures and modern primitive societies, and at various times has been current in central Europe, Asia, Africa and North and South America. It is a credence which lends extra interest to an extraordinary story that was published in the *New York Herald* for 7 September 1871.

Nathan Coker was blacksmith in Easton, Maryland, and had long held the reputation of being immune to heat. A committee of local citizens and members of the press asked if they might put him to the test, and he agreed. First, a shovel was heated in his forge until it became white-hot and incandescent. Coker, we are told, pulled off his boots and placed the hot shovel on the soles of his feet, and kept it there until the shovel became black.

Next, lead shot was heated until molten. Coker swilled it around his teeth and tongue like a mouthwash, until it solidified. Then he plunged his hands into the blazing forge and calmly picked out glowing coals, which he showed to the onlookers on his palms. As a finale, he casually handled a piece of red-hot iron.

'It don't burn,' he told the reporter. 'Since I was a little boy, I've never been afraid to handle fire.'

Coker was neither a showman nor a religious fanatic. To him, the startling phenomenon was simply a fact of life.

Another blacksmith was involved in a similar report made by New York physician Dr K. R. Wissen, in 1927. While on a hunting trip in the Tennessee mountains, the doctor met a shy country boy who could hold burning firebrands without feeling pain or suffering physical injury. The boy told Wissen that he had discovered his mysterious ability as a child, when he had picked up a red-hot horseshoe from a forge. Like Coker, he took his gift entirely for granted.

*The Balinese trance-dancer, **left**, regularly escapes totally unscathed from fire. **The Bible** tells how King Nebuchadnezzar threw three men, as depicted **below**, into the fiery furnace. They, too, emerged unhurt.*

The immunity of certain people to extreme heat – whether cultivated, as in the case of shamanist societies, for instance, or apparently fortuitous, as in the case of such individuals as Nathan Coker – has been a source of wonder and bafflement to observers of the phenomenon for centuries. The very ubiquity, across ages and continents, of these 'human salamanders' adds to the mystery. The Biblical story of Nebuchadnezzar's burning fiery furnace and its three intended victims – Shadrach, Mesach and Abednego – for example, strikes a familiar chord when compared with modern fire-walking in Trinidad or Polynesia. The fire was so hot that it killed the men who put Shadrach and company into it, yet we are told in *Daniel 3, 27*: 'The princes, governors and captains, and the king's counsellors, being gathered together, saw these men, upon whose bodies the fire had no power, nor was an hair of their head singed, neither were their coats changed, nor the smell of fire had passed on to them.'

Classical writers, such as Plato and Virgil, also recorded instances of people walking unscathed on hot coals; while, in the third century AD, the Neoplatonist Porphyry and his pupil Iamblichus

The early 19th-century engraving, right, shows a traditional Thai firewalker, demonstrating his skills. It seems that only 'special' people, those few who are born incombustible, or others who undergo secret magical rites – perhaps involving auto-hypnosis – can expose their flesh to intense heat without feeling or showing any ill-effects.

" AMERICAN PHYSICIST JEARL WALKER DEMONSTRATES THE LEIDENFROST EFFECT BY WETTING HIS FINGERS AND THEN PLUNGING THEM INTO MOLTEN LEAD AT 500° CENTIGRADE. MEAT COOKS AT 100°, BUT THE WET FINGERS ARE PROTECTED, FOR A FEW SECONDS ANYWAY, BY A SHEATH OF WATER VAPOUR. AND HE SUGGESTS THAT THIS COULD BE THE SECRET OF FIRE-WALKING. **"**

LYALL WATSON, LIFETIDE

investigated the phenomenon as part of a thorough and objective survey of divination, spirit-raising and trance states. Certain 'possessed' mediums, they noted, felt no pain and suffered no injury when thrown into, or passed through, fire.

The annals of the early and medieval Church are littered with accounts of such saintly activities as levitation, miracle healing and teleportation, as well as immunity to fire. And though the majority of these are based on hearsay evidence, a handful do stand up to scrutiny. Among them are accounts of 'ordeal by fire', a favourite way of settling ecclesiastical differences. In 1062, the Bishop of Florence was accused by the saintly Peter Aldobrandini of having bribed his way into office. A long, narrow corridor was paved with red hot coals, with a bonfire at each end. Peter walked through one bonfire,

along the coals, and out through the further flames, his flesh and clothing remaining unburned. The Bishop declined to follow him, and resigned instead. Later, in the mid-13th century, another monk with a reputation for holiness, Giovanni Buono, made a habit of demonstrating his faith by shuffling his feet in burning coals 'as if washing them in a brook, for as long as it took to say half a *miserere*'.

In 1637, the French Jesuit, Father Paul Lejeune, was very impressed – although at the same time considerably annoyed – by what he saw among the Huron Indians near Quebec. Lejeune was heading a mission to the Indians, but the tribal medicine men were in no mood to be converted and put on what appeared to be a special show for him – a sort of healing-by-fire ceremony. He wrote:

Firewalking becomes a tourist attraction, above, as holidaymakers eagerly photograph local volunteers stepping out casually over white-hot stones outside the Korolevu Beach Hotel in Fiji.

Saints Alexander and Eventius, right, are joined by Theodulus to celebrate their triumph over the flames into which they were thrown by Aurelius, persecutor of Christians.

An Indian fakir exhibits his technique of mind-over-matter, below, by hanging upside-down over a fire.

'You may believe me, since I speak of a thing that I saw with my own eyes, they [the medicine men] separated the brands, drew the stones from the midst of the fire, and holding their hands behind their back, took them between their teeth, carried them to the patients, and remained some time without loosening their hold . . . not only these persons but even the sick were not burned. They let their bodies be rubbed with glowing cinders without their skin appearing in the least affected.'

Even Lejeune's phlegmatic Jesuitry could not compete and he retired from the scene, temporarily defeated.

In 1731, lay authorities and the Catholic Church joined forces to examine an outbreak of hysterical possession that followed the death of the Jansenist heretic François de Paris four years previously. De Paris' followers, congregating around his grave at St Medard, were reported to have gone into convulsions, during which they spun like tops, twisting their limbs into impossible positions, and levitating. Louis XV ordered the cemetery closed, and appointed a magistrate, Carré de Montgeron (an agnostic), to head the examining board.

One meticulously detailed report compiled by Montgeron, two priests and eight court officials told of the incombustible Marie Souet. Naked, apart from a linen sheet, Marie had gone into a trance that rendered her body rigid. In this condition, she had been suspended over a blazing fire for 35 minutes; and although the flames actually lapped around her, neither she nor the sheet was damaged. The free-thinking Montgeron was so astounded by what he saw that he began a sympathetic examination of spiritism, annoying the authorities and landing himself in the Bastille for his pains.

AFTER-DINNER ENTERTAINMENT

The famous English diarist John Evelyn wrote of seeing 'Richardson the fire-eater' perform after dinner at Lady Sunderland's house in London on 8 October 1672. His account is all the more convincing for the slight note of scepticism at the end:

'He devoured brimstone on glowing coals before us, chewing and swallowing them; he melted a beer glass and ate it quite up; then taking a live coal on his tongue, he put on it a raw oyster, the coal was blown on with bellows till it flamed and sparkled in his mouth, and so remained until the oyster gaped and was quite boiled; then he melted pitch and wax with sulphur, which he drank down as it flamed; I saw it flaming in his mouth a good while. He also took up a thick piece of iron, such as laundresses use to put in their smoothing bokes, when it was fiery hot, held it between his teeth, then in his hand and threw it about like a stone, but this I observed he cared not to hold very long.'

Another celebrated 'after-dinner' performer, whose feats attracted considerable attention in Victorian society, was the medium Daniel Dunglas Home. Lord Adare, an army officer and war correspondent, and H. D. Jencken, a barrister, told how, at a seance in 1868, Home stirred up a glowing fire in the grate and 'placed his face right among the burning coals, moving it about as though bathing it in water'. It seems that Home could confer his immunity to onlookers, too: after making passes over their hands, he would hand them burning embers without them suffering injury. More startlingly, at a seance at the home of Mr and Mrs S. C. Hall, a couple who combined prominence in the art world with membership of the Society for Psychical Research, Home took 'a huge lump of live burning coal, so large that he held it in both hands', and placed it on top of Hall's head. Hall said that the coal felt 'warm but not hot'. According to Mrs Hall, Home 'then proceeded to draw up Mr Hall's white hair over the red coal; Mr Home drew the hair into a sort of pyramid, the coal, still red, showing beneath the hair'.

FIRE-WALKING IN FIJI

Even while Home was startling such establishment figures as Lord Adare and Sir William Crookes, tales of firewalking and firehandling feats from far-flung corners of the Empire were becoming commonplace.

Basil Thompson, for instance, in his *South Sea Yarns*, related how he watched a group of Fijian islanders walking over a long pit of super-heated stones. Thompson put a pocket handkerchief to one of the nearer stones and it immediately scorched; yet not only did the near-naked Fijians walk over the

pit with impunity, but 'their ankle fillets of dry fern remained untouched.'

In 1904, members of Sir Francis Younghusband's expedition to Tibet told of Buddhist monks who could not only stand motionless and unharmed in the midst of blazing fires but sit for hours, clad only in thin saffron robes, in sub-zero temperatures. Over and over again, such stories were told, often by intelligent and unbiased witnesses – only, more often than not, to have them dismissed by the scientific establishment.

Professor E. R. Dodds, in his *Supernormal Phenomena in Classical Antiquity*, outlines the difficulty of collating ancient accounts of paranormal happenings. A useful purpose, he suggests, may be served by examining surviving evidence to see whether the phenomena described are consistent with those from other periods of history. If they are strikingly different, it could be argued that each age is the victim of its own superstitions.

In the case of 'human salamanders', the many similarities between accounts from all ages and countries must mean that the student of the paranormal has a sound basis from which to work.

CLAIRVOYANT DISCOVERIES

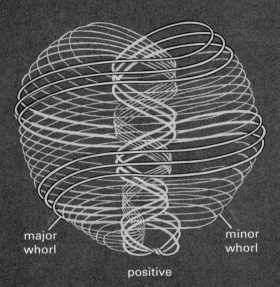

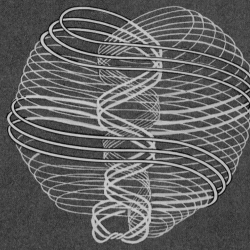

major whorl

minor whorl

positive

negative

The two kinds of ultimate physical atoms, seen clairvoyantly by Annie Besant and C.W. Leadbeater, are shown left. The atoms, which spun incessantly, consisted of currents of energy forming spiral whorls. Colours constantly flashed out, changing according to which spiral was most active.

MODERN PHYSICISTS ARE PROBING EVER DEEPER INTO THE STRUCTURE OF MATTER, USING COSTLY AS WELL AS HIGHLY SOPHISTICATED TECHNOLOGY. HOWEVER, SOME OF THEIR DISCOVERIES MAY HAVE BEEN MADE BEFORE — BY MEANS OF EXTRA-SENSORY PERCEPTION

Annie Besant and Charles Leadbeater, below, are seen working together. Their observations, when viewing matter on the small scale, were in conflict with the science of their time.

Two figures who dominated the Theosophical Society at the end of the 19th century – Annie Besant and Charles W. Leadbeater – began, in 1895, a series of researches that was to last nearly 40 years. They were studying the ultimate structure of matter, using methods that orthodox science did not countenance – attempting to view atoms by means of extra-sensory perception. However, the vast amounts of information they produced seemed to bear no relation to the findings of chemists and physicists during those four decades. Only a century later were resemblances noticed between their descriptions and the modern theory of the structure of fundamental particles. Indeed, it now seems possible that Besant

and Leadbeater saw, by occult means, the 'quarks' that physicists now postulate as the building blocks of matter.

The power of viewing the very small is one of the *siddhis*, (or psychic faculties) that, according to Eastern tradition, can be cultivated by yoga meditation. In the ancient yoga *sutras*, the semi-legendary sage Patanjali lists these: one is the power to gain 'knowledge of the small, the hidden, or the distant by directing the light of a superphysical faculty'.

*In*Focus

WINDOWS ON THE WHORLS

The diagrams of *micro-psi* atoms drawn from the descriptions provided by the two Theosophists – Annie Besant and Charles Leadbeater – give only a faint impression of the fantastic spectacles they witnessed. But what they saw was also confirmed by later clairvoyants using *micro-psi* (the faculty of viewing the very small) in the late 1950s. Initially, a mist or haze of light would appear when they observed matter on the microscopic scale. With greater magnification, the mist would then become resolved into myriad points of light, they said. These were viewed by them as scintillating and moving chaotically. Some atoms moved in regular orbits, forming the seven minor and three major whorls of the atoms. Some cascaded, rather like showers of meteors. But the motion of the atoms was said to be confined to well-defined volumes of space, in any one of seven different geometric forms. Each 'ultimate physical atom' was enclosed in a 'bubble', as if some sort of transparent membrane was surrounding it. The Theosophists even spoke of space itself being pushed back by the dynamic activity of the matter in the atom. This accorded with the complex theories of Theosophy, which hold that what we normally regard as a vacuum is only one of the seven states of matter.

This ability to acquire knowledge of the small or microscopic is sometimes termed *micro-psi;* and Besant and Leadbeater claimed to have gained their *micro-psi* abilities under the tutelage of their Indian gurus.

To acquire knowledge paranormally that is confirmed by conventional science only years later is perhaps the most convincing type of ESP. In such cases, there is no possibility that the psychic has access to established sources of information. And whether or not the ESP was exercised under controlled laboratory conditions, it is impossible, in principle, to have gained such information either by fraud or by means of the five senses.

The atom of hydrogen, below left, according to Besant and Leadbeater, was a transparent egg-shaped body containing smaller globes arranged in two interlinked triangles. Each one of the globes contained three of the 'ultimate physical atoms'.

The shapes, below right, are the seven fundamental forms of the micro-psi atoms, discovered by the Theosophists.

In 1895, Annie Besant and Charles Leadbeater went so far as to publish pictures of what they claimed were hydrogen, nitrogen and oxygen atoms present in the air. According to a description, given in their book *Occult Chemistry*, a hydrogen atom was:

'Seen to consist of six small bodies, contained in an egg-like form... It rotated with great rapidity on its own axis, vibrating at the same time, the internal bodies performing similar gyrations. The whole atom spins and quivers and has to be steadied before exact observation is possible. The six little bodies are arranged in two sets of three, forming two triangles that are not interchangeable.'

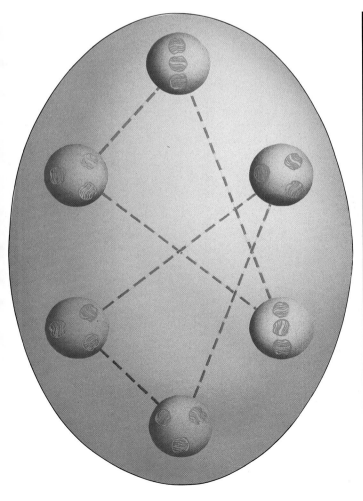

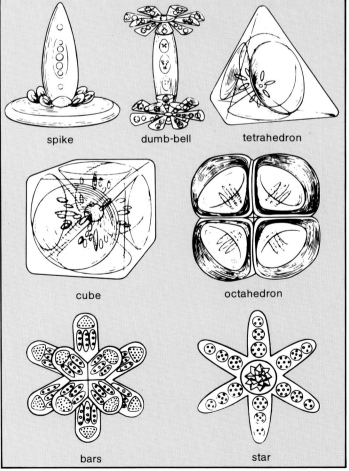

spike   dumb-bell   tetrahedron

cube   octahedron

bars   star

But these 'six little bodies' were not the most basic units of matter. The psychics could magnify the images of them and found that each was composed of a globe enclosing three 'points of light'. When these, in turn, were highly magnified, they appeared as particles of definite size. Besant and Leadbeater called them 'ultimate physical atoms'.

Each of these 'ultimate' particles was seen to be made up of 10 convoluted spiral curves, or whorls, three of which (known as the 'major' whorls) appeared thicker or brighter than the other seven ('minor') whorls. The overall form of the whorls was that of a heart, with one end slightly concave and the other end pointed.

ATOMIC STRUCTURE

The Theosophists' description of matter differed greatly from the contemporary scientific notions of the atom. Two centuries earlier, Sir Isaac Newton (1642-1726), the great English physicist, had conjectured that atoms were 'solid, massy, impenetrable'. By 1895, however, it was suspected that atoms did have a structure and that they were composed of smaller electrically charged particles. One of these, it was believed, was an electron, a negatively charged particle much lighter than an atom. Electric currents were thought to consist of electrons in motion. Then, in 1897, the electron's existence was demonstrated by the English physicist J. J. Thomson. Various models of the structure of the atom were then proposed. But the theory that finally won acceptance, as the result of the experimental and theoretical analyses of the physicists H. Geiger, E. Marsden and Lord Rutherford, was that of the 'nuclear' atom. It showed that the electrons in an atom orbit a tiny nucleus in which all the atom's positive charge and most of its mass are concentrated. When this was first demonstrated, from 1909 onwards, the electrons were supposed to move in well-defined orbits, rather like those of the planets. They were thought to whirl around the nucleus millions of times per second, in a volume with a ten-millionth of the breadth of a pinhead. Then, in the 1920s, with the advent of quantum mechanics (the theory of atomic structure), the electrons and their orbits came to be regarded as 'fuzzy' and ill-defined.

As each scientific picture of the atom was discarded and replaced by the next, Besant and Leadbeater continued to produce remarkably consistent descriptions of their *micro-psi* atoms, which at no time bore any resemblance to the atoms of the orthodox scientists.

Nevertheless, the two Theosophists observed, in 1908, that in certain elements – for example, the inert gases neon, argon, krypton and xenon and the metal platinum – the atoms were not all identical. Neon, for example, had a variant they called *meta-neon*, which had a different atomic weight. This anticipated, by almost six years, the scientific realisation that chemically indistinguishable variants of an element could exist, having atoms of different weights. These variants in turn came to be called 'isotopes'.

One of the most important tools of orthodox chemistry is the periodic table. This is a classification of the elements in terms of their chemical

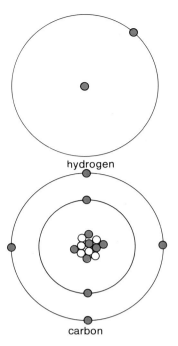

hydrogen

carbon

In conventional science, the nucleus of the hydrogen atom, top, comprises a single positively charged proton. The nuclei of heavier atoms, such as carbon, above, consist of protons and neutral particles called neutrons. Negatively charged electrons orbit the nucleus.

Isotopes of an element such as neon, below, have equal numbers of protons but different numbers of neutrons.

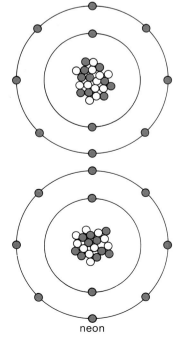

neon

properties and their atomic weights. The atomic weights of the elements increase as you read across the table from left to right, and down it, from top to bottom. Chemical properties change systematically along each row of the table and down each column. Besant and Leadbeater found that the complex shape of the *micro-psi* atom corresponded to the column of the periodic table in which that element lay.

When the psychics began their research, between 60 and 70 elements were known (of the 90 or so that occur in nature) and there were many gaps in the periodic table. Besant and Leadbeater described a number of types of *micro-psi* atom that corresponded, they believed, to gaps in the table. The existence of these elements, and many of their properties, could have been predicted by science, but had not yet been observed.

The atoms that the two psychics described were sometimes seen to be combined into larger units, just as the corresponding chemical atoms combined into larger groupings, called molecules. The *micro-psi* atoms were combined in the same number as the atoms known to science. But, in total violation of all that was known to chemistry, *micro-psi* atoms were observed to be broken up and their constituent particles mixed with those of other atoms. Sceptics felt that this discredited Besant and Leadbeater's claims, since chemical atoms do not split up and mix with each other wholesale when they combine, though they share or transfer some outer electrons.

Other problems emerged. For example, Leadbeater described the *micro-psi* molecule of the compound benzene as being octahedral – that is, as having the overall shape of an eight-faced solid. But chemists already knew that the chemical molecule of benzene was flat and hexagonal. And the psychics described *micro-psi* atoms of several supposed elements for which there was no room whatever in the periodic table

Such problems as these add up to overwhelming evidence against the two Theosophists' interpretation of the *micro-psi* atoms as being the atoms studied by the chemist. Neither could they have been the nuclei of atoms, which do not split up in chemical reactions. What, then, were they? If they were merely hallucinations, why should the forms described by Besant and Leadbeater have correlated with the position of the element in the periodic table? How could the two psychics have 'guessed' that some atoms exist in different forms five years before scientists suspected the existence of isotopes? These aspects of their work remain mysterious even today.

 TO ACQUIRE KNOWLEDGE PARANORMALLY THAT IS CONFIRMED BY CONVENTIONAL SCIENCE ONLY YEARS LATER IS PERHAPS THE MOST CONVINCING TYPE OF ESP. *"*

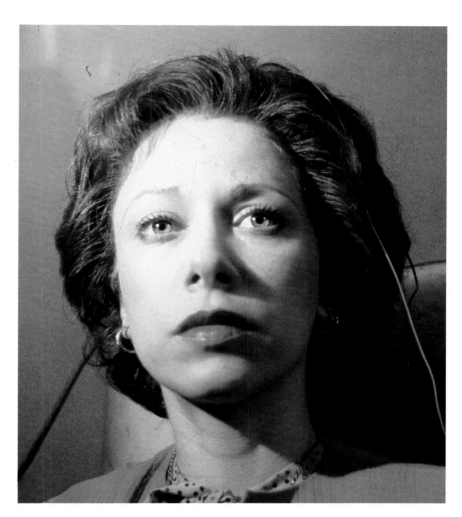

What is 'reality' and what are dreams? To the scientist, things are only real when they can be communicated by the senses or by instruments that are extensions of the senses, when their measurements can be taken and their behaviour observed, when deductions can be made about them and scientific laws subsequently established. In the realms of thought, sane men also distinguish, mainly without difficulty, between fantasies and 'real' concepts.

But research has shown that there are, indeed, 'realities' beyond those generally perceived by our five senses, such as notes with a pitch too high to be heard by human ears. And there may be yet another form of 'reality', confirmed by the experiences

STALKED BY NIGHTMARES

Actress Connie Booth, above, played the principal role in the BBC's dramatised documentary The Story of Ruth *in 1982. Ruth, an American living in London with her husband Paul, was of average intelligence and perfectly normal – except for one thing: a three-dimensional hallucination of her father (who was still resident in the USA) followed and tormented her, reviving the hell she had been through when, as a 10-year-old, she had been sexually molested by him, as shown in the still,* left.

of mystics while in their ecstasies. But the fact remains that 'sanity' for most of us is the common ground of shared sensory perception: on the whole, the cat sits on the mat and not vice versa.

But what if our minds betray us, not in casual mistakes but by completely misinterpreting data supplied by our senses? What of Sybil Isabel Dorsett who, among her 16 personalities, saw herself in the mirror variously as a sophisticated blonde, brown-haired, a tall, willowy redhead, a dark, brown-eyed man, a blue-eyed man, a timid ash-blonde, a small, slim brunette – and with widely differing characters to match. She even bought clothes to suit one personality that would be utterly unsuitable for her 'real' physical self, the choice later utterly bewildering her other selves when they inhabited her body.

And what of Ruth, a 25-year-old American woman, married to Paul and living in London with their three children, the patient of Dr Morton Schatzman, psychiatrist? Her experiences are narrated in Schatzman's book, *The Story of Ruth*, dramatised on television by the BBC in 1982.

Ruth described her symptoms to Dr Schatzman: sex with Paul seemed 'dirty', she was scared of doors, avoided company, panicked in crowds and hated going shopping; she had no appetite, felt negative towards her children, and sensed that her brain was going to explode. She had been the third in a family of four, the youngest being 10 years her junior. While her mother was having the last baby, Ruth's father attempted to rape her – and nearly succeeded. That the assault was likely to have been real, not imagined, is supported by the fact that the father was an habitual drunkard and regularly took drugs. He was also violent – once he actually fired a gun at Ruth (but missed); he had forged cheques; and he was a frequent inmate of mental homes and jails.

SICKENING HATRED

Ruth told her mother about her father's assault, but she professed not to believe her daughter, and packed her off immediately to the children's home where she had lived whenever her father deserted the family. Ruth married at 17, never lived with her parents again and felt a 'sickening hatred' towards her father.

What Ruth did not immediately tell Schatzman was that, almost every day, she had seen an hallucination of her father that appeared as real and solid as any living person. He had begun to appear a year after the birth of her youngest child. Sometimes she saw his face superimposed on Paul's or on her baby's; and even when she did not see him, she felt his presence in the house. She believed he wanted her dead and was prompting her to suicide. Once he sat with her at a friend's dining table, and looked so solid and ordinary that, if Ruth had been at home, she felt she would have offered him coffee. On another occasion, he occupied a chair between two visitors. She heard him speaking and watched him following their conversation – although he was invisible and inaudible to the others present.

Ruth became an in-patient at the Arbours Crisis Centre set up by Dr Schatzman and colleagues in London in 1971. There, she continued to see her

There are many legends in which hapless victims are pursued – and sometimes confronted – by paranormal beings, ghosts or, perhaps, hallucinations. The most famous of these were the Furies of Greek legend, who hounded Orestes, below. Ruth's 'father' pursued her as relentlessly as the Furies, mocking her terror, stalking her as she walked down the street, or suddenly appearing among a group of friends. He persecuted her in this way, she believed, because he thought that when she was a child he 'hadn't hurt her enough'.

❚❚ THAT FOURTH TIME – IT WAS ABOUT 12 NOON – SHE SAW A MAN SITTING IN FRONT OF HER ON THE TRAIN CHANGE INTO HER FATHER. SHE BECAME FRIGHTENED. WHEN SHE REACHED HER STOP AND GOT OFF THE TRAIN. THE MAN GOT OFF TOO, BEHIND HER. HE HAD HER FATHER'S FORM. SHE HOPED HE WOULD WALK IN A DIFFERENT DIRECTION, BUT HE DID NOT. SHE RAN TO A PHONE AT THE STATION TO CALL THE CRISIS CENTRE TO ASK SOMEONE TO MEET HER. **❚❚**

DR MORTON SCHATZMAN

father. She even felt her bed moved by his legs knocking against it (although it did not actually move). She saw him very clearly – 'I can see each tooth' – heard him laughing and even smelt the sweat on him while in the doctor's presence.

Schatzman saw that Ruth thought rationally: her overall pattern of behaviour was not that of a psychotic, and he knew that it was statistically common for mentally healthy people in the West to have some experience of hallucinations. Having read that the Senoi, a Malayan tribe, thought dream life so important that they taught children to face, master and use whatever caused terror in their

Guilt, in the form of the apparition of a 'wronged lady', is said to have warned Lord Lyttleton, as depicted left, of his approaching death.

nightmares, he suggested to Ruth that she follow their example and confront her father's apparition.

The victory was not immediately, nor easily won, however. Ruth continued to see her father, sometimes superimposed even on to complete strangers, and to hear and smell him. She also felt that he read her thoughts and sensed that he was trying to master her and take her over. The psychiatrist told her to send the apparition packing, which she eventually did on occasions – but sometimes his distinctive smell remained.

FATHER FIGURE

On her sixth day at the centre, Ruth saw Paul change into her father; and when he lightly touched her hand, she felt it squeezed until it hurt. She refused to sleep with her husband that night because she felt he was her father. The next day, she saw her father's face superimposed upon Dr Schatzman's. The doctor had suggested that she try to change him into her father because confronting something usually makes one fear it less and it would prove to Ruth that she had control: if she could summon the apparition at will, she could also

▮▮ RUTH NEXT DOUBLED DR SCHATZMAN IN HIS PRESENCE – CREATING, IN EFFECT, HIS DOPPELGÄNGER SITTING IN A CHAIR ON HIS LEFT. WHEN SCHATZMAN WENT TO SIT IN HIS DOUBLE'S CHAIR, THE LATTER SAT IN HIS . . . SHE SAW BOTH MEN, REFLECTED SIMULTANEOUSLY IN A MIRROR. ▮▮

In a scene from the television drama, below, Ruth feels repelled by Paul's sexual advances – for it was not her husband (played by Colin Bruce) whom she saw lying beside her, but her father. Later in the course of her treatment, she found she could not only summon up an hallucination of Paul when he was absent, but actually make love with the hallucination – an experience she found to be sexually satisfying.

will it away. This achieved, the next step was to create the illusion without using a real body as a 'model', and dismiss it: this she managed to do.

Further advance was made when Ruth again superimposed her father on to Schatzman, but he appeared to be wearing different clothes from the doctor. When Schatzman moved towards her, the apparition did so too; and when Schatzman lightly laid his hand upon Ruth's, she again felt her hand being painfully squeezed. She succeeded in dismissing the appearance, but the experience left her very tired.

When Ruth left the centre after 11 days, Schatzman suggested that, far from being 'crazy', she was gifted in being able to summon and dismiss apparitions at will. Her family history suggested to him that the gift might be hereditary. At this point, the doctor had to go to New York for two-and-a-half weeks, during which time Ruth's father appeared to her at least eight times. She heard the rustle of his clothes and the popping of his cigarettes out of a packet, and was awoken once when he sat on her bed. She managed to send him away once, confused him on another occasion by casual reference to coffee and on a third, when he appeared while she was having a bath, asked him to pass her a towel. The apparition subsequently ceased for 19 days, its longest continuous absence, but then suddenly reappeared, superimposed upon Paul in bed.

On his return, Schatzman suggested that Ruth should try to create a friendlier apparition as an experiment in control. After some effort, she projected a complete image of her best friend Becky, and held mental conversations with her. Ruth's apparitions usually behaved normally (although occasionally they walked through closed doors), but she also hallucinated the consequences of their actions, feeling a draught of air through a door opened by them and seeing Becky squeezing toothpaste on to a brush and handing it to her, though the door, paste and brush had not really moved. The duration of the appearances varied

from seconds to 15 or 20 minutes, and their creation both excited and drained her. She found that her apparitions also had personalities: although she could finally dismiss them, she could not always make them do what they did not want to do.

Ruth next 'doubled' Dr Schatzman in his presence – creating, in effect, his doppelgänger sitting in a chair on his left. When Schatzman went to sit in his double's chair, the latter sat in his, and when he passed in front of the apparition, he blocked it from Ruth's sight. She saw both men, reflected simultaneously in a mirror; and when Dr Schatzman held out his arms to thin air, Ruth saw him actually dance with his double!

Ruth made further progress when she produced an apparition of herself with which she established mental communication, although she found the experience exhausting. She repeated the experiment in Dr Schatzman's presence, her head hurting and heart pounding with all the effort this involved.

A TWILIGHT WORLD

By this time, in many respects Ruth had changed from patient to co-researcher with the psychiatrist. When she observed that an apparition's legs cast a shadow, experiments were carried out with light and darkness. Ruth could hallucinate the darkening and lighting-up of a room, yet failed to be able to make out the words on a bookcover in a room that was actually dark but which she 'saw' as lit. She could walk round an apparition, viewing it from every angle, could feel it (it was, she said, a little colder than a living being), and could see and feel it moving parts of her body, though these did not really move, or only very slightly. The apparitions could write messages that Ruth was also able to read, but the paper remained blank to everyone else, and they did not appear in photographs of chairs in which she saw them, nor did their voices

... SHE SAT ON THE FLOOR AND ASKED ME TO SIT ON A CHAIR BEHIND HER AND NEAR HER. THAT WAY, SHE COULD SEE MY REFLECTION IN THE MIRROR IF SHE NEEDED TO. IT WAS FOR HER SECURITY, SHE SAID. IF HER FATHER'S FACE APPEARED TO REPLACE HER FACE, THEN HER FATHER MIGHT TAKE OVER HER BEING, IN WHICH CASE SHE WANTED ME NEARBY. *■■*

DR MARTIN SCHATZMAN

register on tape recorders – thus proving they had no objective reality.

Ruth next discovered she could create her father's apparition superimposed upon her own reflection in a mirror, and did so with Dr Schatzman sitting by to prevent her being 'taken over'. She 'felt' her father's emotions and this frightened her. 'He', in reply to the psychiatrist's questions, gave information about himself. For Ruth, the experiment resulted in considerable discomfort; but, although she felt her father's fear, anger and sexual desire, she was not taken over by him. The experience involved similarities to mediumistic trances. However, whether the information that was given by her 'father' was true – and whether Ruth had ever known it – could not be determined.

Dr Morton Schatzman, above left, the psychiatrist, had an imaginative and sympathetic approach to Ruth's distress and finally eradicated the nightmare element from the hallucinations she saw, actually helping her control and even create them at will.

Ruth is seen, left, confiding in Dr Schatzman, played by Peter Whitman, in the BBC television programme.

During several such sessions, a number of facts connected with her father's previous history and Ruth's childhood emerged. She seemed to feel his and her own emotions simultaneously, and the more she learned about him, the more she pitied him. She also found she could create him and merge with him without using the mirror, and still sense his feelings as before. 'The more I relaxed,' she said, 'the less I saw him and the more I became him.' Schatzman discovered that he could talk directly to the father through Ruth and found a plausible personality consistent with itself but not with Ruth's. Schatzman wondered whether this personality could have been a buried aspect of herself.

A startling development occurred when Ruth visited the USA and spent some time with her

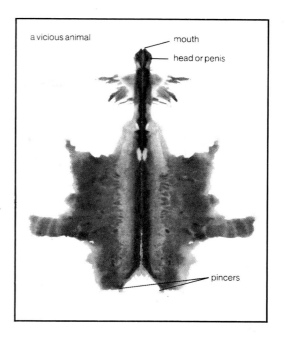

a vicious animal — mouth
— head or penis
— pincers

Psychiatrists frequently make use of Rorschach inkblot tests to gain some insight into the minds of their patients. The tests use randomly produced inkblots; and patients are asked what the shapes remind them of. Ruth, both as her adult self and when hypnotically regressed to her teens, was shown several such inkblots. One, left, was shown to the 'teenage' Ruth, who saw in it the heads of two babies, both of whom were bleeding. At another session, she saw two old women and a vagina in the same inkblot – an identification that anyone might make. The other blot reproduced, right, reminded the hypnotised Ruth of a vicious animal with pincers – or a penis. Asked if she had ever seen her father's penis, the 'teenage' Ruth replied primly: 'No, never. He was very careful never to do that sort of thing.' Yet when the notes of the session were read back to her 'normal' self, Ruth said that was a lie: 'He would wave it at you when he was drunk.' What seems to have emerged from these sessions was that the 'teenage' Ruth had disliked psychiatrists intensely and so said anything in order to be as uncooperative as possible. Her general level of association when faced with the inkblots was certainly not that of a psychotic.

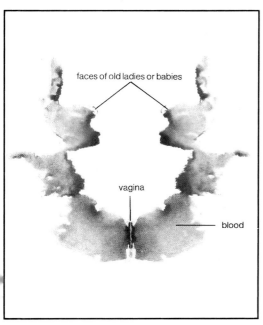

faces of old ladies or babies

vagina

blood

father there. She created an apparition of Paul in her car – what is more, her father apparently also saw it. Perhaps even more startling was her success in twice making love with apparitions of Paul whom she 'created' on nights when he was absent. Both experiences were, she reported, sexually very satisfying.

Other experiments, however, failed. For example, Ruth tried to describe some new underpants Paul had bought by envisaging his apparition clad in them – but they were not the same as the real ones. And in an attempt to elicit information about Dr Schatzman's life from his apparition, the 'misses' far outweighed the 'hits'.

Gradually, the limits of Ruth's strange ability were revealed. But she actually succeeded in making a double of herself. This doppelgänger – which brought to her recollection forgotten incidents from her youth – may simply have been a mechanism that enabled her to tap into subliminal memories. Whatever the explanation, Ruth recalled incidents from her past in great detail, many of which were later confirmed by her mother. Sometimes, she could even merge with her own apparition, so that she would enter 'memory trances', which in some respects were like those of spirit mediums and in others like hypnotic regression. In time, she learned

to use this 'trance' technique without having to create her double, but did need someone else to be present in order to tell her what she had said, because she would not remember it.

In her regressions, Ruth talked and behaved like a child or an adolescent. Given a number of psychological tests while regressed to various ages, she performed in them as girls of those ages would be expected to do, thereby showing that she was reliving her past. Other tests proved that Ruth's apparitions affected her sight and hearing exactly as flesh and blood entities would have done. Dr Schatzman concluded that, far from being 'crazy' or having a damaged brain, Ruth showed evidence of an extraordinary capacity for creativity and projection.

Why, then, did the hallucinations come when they did? In 1976, when they began, her elder daughter was three years old – the age at which Ruth first entered the children's home – and her eldest child was seven, her age when her father returned to the family after his first period of desertion. These recollections of childhood traumas, perhaps subconscious, allied to the loneliness of living overseas in England – another Ruth amid the alien corn – could well have triggered her experiences.

And what of Ruth after the therapy? Her apparitions were to become pure entertainment. When driving alone, for instance, she found she could put one in the passenger seat for company, or converse with another, silently, at a boring party. The implications of her story for psychical research are far-reaching indeed.

> **DR SCHATZMAN CONCLUDED THAT, FAR FROM BEING CRAZY OR HAVING A DAMAGED BRAIN, RUTH SHOWED EVIDENCE OF AN EXTRAORDINARY CAPACITY FOR CREATIVITY AND PROJECTION.**

SCIENCE AND THE

DREAM-MAKERS

PSYCHOLOGISTS STUDYING DREAMS IN THE EXPERIMENTAL LABORATORY HAVE FOUND NOTABLE EXAMPLES OF TELEPATHY AND PRECOGNITION. BUT IS IT POSSIBLE TO PRODUCE DREAM ESP TO ORDER?

The painting of Luis Angel Firpo knocking Jack Dempsey out of the ring, above, was transmitted telepathically to a sleeper, triggering a dream about boxing.

Dr Montague Ullman is seen below, monitoring the brain waves of a sleeper in his dream laboratory.

The artist's dream puzzled him. It had begun with images of a number of posts. Then he had the impression of a prize fight. 'I had to go to Madison Square Gardens to pick up tickets to a boxing fight,' he recalled, 'and there were a lot of tough punks around – people connected with the fight around the place.' Why should he have such a dream? He had no interest in boxing, and had never even been to a fight.

Surprisingly, however, there was a reason for the dream. The artist was a guinea pig in the dream laboratory at the Maimonides Medical Center, at the State University of New York. He had allowed himself to be wired up to a machine that monitors brain activity during sleep. As soon as it registered a reading showing that he had entered a stage of

REM (rapid eye movement) sleep and that he was therefore dreaming, the researchers woke him up and asked him to describe his dream.

In another part of the Maimonides laboratory, meanwhile, a woman was looking at a picture that had been chosen at random from a pool of 12, and was concentrating on trying to communicate it to the sleeping artist. The target picture on this occasion was a painting that showed Jack Dempsey being knocked out of the ring at Madison Square Gardens. When independent judges were shown a verbal description of the sleeper's dream impressions, together with the 12 pictures in the target pool, they had no difficulty in matching it with the painting of Dempsey's fight. The dream was a spectacular telepathic hit.

TRANSMITTED PICTURES

Such experiments at the Maimonides dream laboratory were conducted for over 15 years from the early 1960s, and were designed specifically to look for telepathy between dreaming subjects and agents who set out to 'transmit' pictures to them. They found one particularly good subject, Dr William Erwin, and an equally good agent, Sol Feldstein, who was a doctoral student; and the research team were able to conduct telepathy-in-dream experiments with them that yielded results far better than chance could be expected to produce. (The odds were in fact 1,000 to 1 against chance being responsible.)

But, every so often, the researchers came upon cases where, instead of receiving someone else's thoughts, a dreamer would apparently have a glimpse of the future. This came as no surprise to Dr Montague Ullman, the New York psychiatrist who led the Maimonides team. He had himself experienced a premonition in one of his dreams.

One night, Ullman dreamed that he met fellow dream researcher, Dr Krippner, and was surprised to see that he had a massive, bleeding lesion on his face. The dream startled him so much that he awoke 'with a sinking sense of terror'. Later that day, Ullman visited a part of New York City with which he was unfamiliar. There, he was surprised to see a man whose walk – 'a kind of hunched shuffle' – reminded him of Krippner.

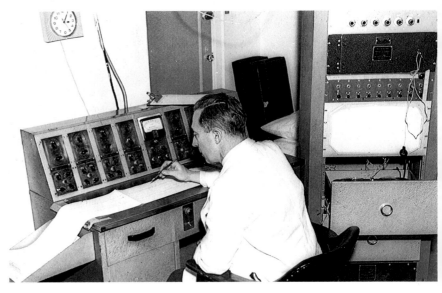

In a major experiment in mass telepathy, a rock band, the Grateful Dead, enlisted their audiences as 'senders'. The 'receiver' was Malcolm Bessent, above, who slept at the dream laboratory. One night, the audience 'sent' the picture of the seven spinal chakras, right. In yoga, these are claimed to be bodily energy centres. Bessent's dream description referred to using natural energy; an 'energy box' to catch sunlight; someone levitating; and a spinal column. Note the figure's halo, which could well have stimulated the idea of sunlight.

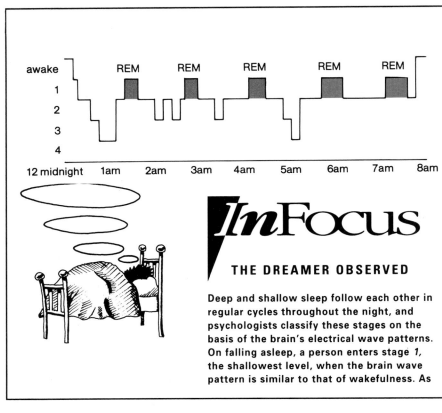

*In*Focus

THE DREAMER OBSERVED

Deep and shallow sleep follow each other in regular cycles throughout the night, and psychologists classify these stages on the basis of the brain's electrical wave patterns. On falling asleep, a person enters stage *1*, the shallowest level, when the brain wave pattern is similar to that of wakefulness. As sleep deepens into stages *2, 3* and *4,* the brain waves become slower, though their voltage increases. Some muscles, such as those of the limbs and the jaw, relax while others, such as those that push food along the digestive tract, continue normally. After about one-and-a-half hours, brain waves suddenly return to the stage *1* pattern, while the body becomes yet more relaxed and completely immobile – except for the eyes, which begin quick, jerky movements behind the closed eyelids. It is difficult to rouse the sleeper from this REM (rapid eye movement) sleep; but when this is done, the sleeper nearly always has a dream to report, which may be vivid and full of action. Typically, REM sleep lasts about 20 minutes; the whole cycle is then repeated. Later cycles are shallower than earlier ones. Volunteers contributing to dream experiments have been deprived of their dreams, however, by being woken when REM begins. Even after months of this, there is usually little effect on waking life, but the volunteers compensate by spending much more of the night dreaming as soon as this is again permitted by the experimenters.

Convinced that it was his colleague, but puzzled that he should also be in that part of the city, Ullman crossed the road to speak to him. As he approached, however, he realised it was not Krippner – but the man had 'the same, horrible, ulcerating lesion around his mouth' that he had seen in his dream the night before.

This was a spontaneous dream experience, but Ullman found the same shift in time occurring in the laboratory, too. In early 1971, a rock band, the Grateful Dead, took an interest in the Maimonides telepathy research and visited the dream laboratory. The research team decided to enlist the musicians' help in an experiment designed to discover whether telepathic communication is stronger if more than one agent is involved. The band was giving six concerts in New York, 45 miles (70 kilometres) from the research unit, and agreed to ask each night's 2,000-strong audience to act as telepathic 'agents'.

On the evening of each concert, an English psychic, Malcolm Bessent, went to sleep at the Maimonides laboratory, under the watchful eye of the research team. At each concert, a picture of Bessent would then be projected briefly on to a screen. Then another picture, selected at random, was shown for 15 minutes, while the Grateful Dead played their music, and the audience tried to transmit the picture.

When Bessent's dreams were analysed, it was found that he had succeeded in scoring four 'hits' out of six. And the story does not end there: indeed, it has an unexpected twist. The researchers wondered if it would be possible for someone to 'intercept' the telepathic communication and describe the pictures. They therefore asked another of their laboratory subjects, Felicia Parise, to try to tune into the concert audience's thoughts, but the audience was not told she was doing so. Taken at face value, her results were disappointing, because there was only one 'hit'. But the team noticed a remarkable displacement effect.

On three nights, Felicia Parise's impressions bore no resemblance at all to the picture that was being shown to the audience at that time: instead, they were impressive descriptions of images that either had been shown to the audience on earlier nights or were still to be randomly chosen and projected. She seems somehow to have seen into both the past and the future.

Psychical researchers have long been aware that dreams provide a wealth of paranormal information. There were apparently many dream warnings of the Aberfan disaster of 1966, when 144 people died in a tiny Welsh village as the result of a coal tip subsiding. When Dr John Barker analysed 31 supposed premonitions of the tragedy, he found that 28 had occurred in dreams.

Until the 1950s, the problem for investigators of dream premonitions was that most people have no recollection of their dreams, or rapidly forget them. But then it was found that, by waking a person after a period of 'rapid eye movement' sleep, an account of a dream was almost always forthcoming. The technique also enabled researchers to time 'transmission' of mental images to a sleeper to coincide with a dreaming phase.

Dreams vary in nature, and studies of one kind in particular – lucid dreams – are currently exciting a great deal of interest. The name might suggest merely a particularly vivid dream, but the term is in fact used to describe experiences in which the sleeper knows he is dreaming and can look at his dream objectively, even critically, and perhaps even control its content.

Lucid dreams have been the subject of study and discussion for many years. As early as 1896, a

Dutch investigator, Dr van Eeden, began recording his dreams; and, after three years, started to distinguish lucid dreams from the others, recording 352 in all. The following had a particular impact:

'In May 1903, I dreamed that I was in a little provincial Dutch town and at once encountered my brother-in-law, who had died some time before. I was absolutely sure that it was he, and I knew that he was dead... He told me that a financial catastrophe was impending for me. Somebody was going to rob me of a sum of 10,000 guilders. I said that I understood him, though after waking up I was utterly puzzled by it and could make nothing of it... I wish to point out that this was the only prediction I ever received in a lucid dream in such an impressive way. It came only too true – with this difference, that the sum I lost was 20 times greater. At

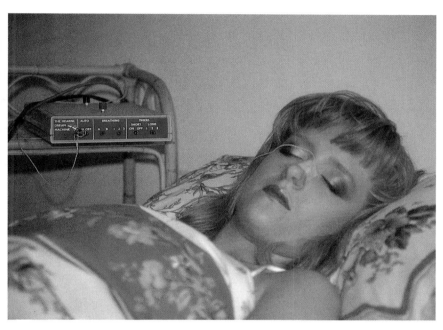

Dr Keith Hearne's dream machine, above, uses a nose-clip to monitor breathing. When the rate and depth of breathing show a lucid dream is possible, weak electrical shocks indicating the fact are delivered to the subject, who can then become the director of his or her own 'dream movie'.

the time of the dream, there seemed not to be the slightest probability of such a catastrophe. I was not even in possession of the money I lost afterwards. Yet it was just the time when the first events took place – the railway strikes of 1903 – that led up to my financial ruin.'

Dr Keith Hearne, author of *Visions of the Future* and *The Dream Machine*, is pioneering a new approach to dream research through lucid dreaming, and coupling his study with experiments in the nature of ESP. When a sleeping person is dreaming, not only does he experience rapid eye movements, but his muscles become virtually paralysed. So, even though the dreamer is having a lucid dream and therefore knows he is dreaming, he cannot signal this fact to the researcher by, for example, switching a button, because his fingers will not move. Hearne therefore decided to see if communication could take place between sleeper and researcher using eye movements as signals.

By pre-arrangement with subjects, it was agreed that eight left-right movements of the eyes would indicate that a lucid dream was happening at that moment. The first such communication was recorded in April 1975 at the dream laboratory at Hull University, where Hearne was working at the time.

AT THE MOMENT THAT THE PERIOD OF DREAM LUCIDITY STARTS, A TRANSFORMATION TAKES PLACE: IT IS AS IF CONSCIOUSNESS HAS BEEN SUDDENLY SWITCHED ON... THE ARTIFICIALITY OF THE DREAM SURROUNDINGS IS REALIZED, BUT THE REALNESS IS SO STRIKING THAT THE WHOLE EXPERIENCE CAN BE ONE OF SHEER WONDERMENT.

DR KEITH HEARNE

Since then, such communication has become more sophisticated. Using pre-arranged codes, subjects can signal that they are flying, or have just landed, or are performing some other deliberate act.

Early work proved laborious, however: after spending 45 nights in the laboratory, Hearne had recorded only eight lucid dreams. So he went on to devise a 'dream machine' that provides 'conscious controllable dreams'. It detects that a sleeper has begun to dream and then signals to the sleeper by applying a small voltage to his wrist. The sleeping mind thereby knows that it is dreaming, and the dream becomes a lucid one.

DREAM TELEPATHY

Hearne also discovered that a lucid dreamer can signal to the waking world by altering his breathing pattern, and has used this fact in a novel way in order to test ESP. When a sleeper realises he is dreaming, he makes rapid breathing movements. A bedside black box responds to this and immediately sets off an automatic dialling machine. When the other participant in the experiment receives a telephone call and there is silence on the line, he or she knows that the subject is having a lucid dream at that moment. A picture card is then selected at random by the recipient of the call and a mental picture is sent to the dreamer, just as in the telepathy experiments at Maimonides Medical Center. Hearne's work on ESP in lucid dreams continues, and further results are eagerly awaited.

Since ancient times, dreams have been regarded as channels of occult or otherwise extraordinary knowledge. It may indeed be that, in the dreaming state, human beings are at their most sensitive to the most subtle of influences impinging on them – from other minds, from the wider Universe, and even from the past and future. Experimental scrutiny of psychic activity during dreaming has begun, and seems to suggest that a great advance in our understanding of this aspect of the paranormal is imminent. As Keith Hearne says: 'Lucid dreams are the ideal state for testing *psi* because the dreamer knows he is dreaming and is taking part in a *psi* experiment. Lucid dreams may well be the royal road to a knowledge of psychic phenomena.'

SQUATTERS IN THE MIND

CERTAIN INDIVIDUALS SEEM TO POSSESS A HOST OF DIFFERENT SELVES THAT COME AND GO CONTINUALLY. WHAT LIES BEHIND SUCH CASES OF FLUID AND UNCERTAIN IDENTITY?

The history of Man's advance since the medieval period has been the story of his gradual realisation of how little he seems to matter in the scheme of things. From the pre-Copernican view that he lived at the centre of the Universe – a Universe that was not very much larger than the Earth – he has been forced by modern astronomical discoveries to accept that the Earth is but an insignificant dot in the Galaxy, while the Galaxy, in relation to the visible Universe, is the size of a speck of dust in a cathedral. His fond conceit that he was 'Lord of Creation' over the beasts of the field has been swept away by Darwin and his

Are such creatures as those in **The Sleep of Reason Brings Forth Monsters,** *by Goya,* above, *the products of our own unconscious minds – or are they sometimes intruders from outside? Evidence suggests that our minds may not in fact enjoy undisputed possession of our bodies.*
In **The Three Faces of Eve,** *Joanne Woodward,* right, *played a multiple personality victim, with one self who behaved uninhibitedly.*

successors: indeed, to many, he seems simply to be an animal species that grew a large brain and is now in serious danger of following both the dinosaur and the dodo to extinction. In the 19th century, his assumption that he was at least in charge of his mind, overseeing its workings and guiding it according to rational purposes, was also undermined by Freud's theories of the subconscious. Freud discovered that large tracts of Man's thinking processes lay behind a barrier. Often, decisions were taken there and then surfaced: thus, in implementing them, Man was cast more in the role of public relations officer than of managing director.

Notwithstanding such withdrawals to more modest estimates of his position, Man could still console himself with the belief that, at any rate, his mental processes, conscious and unconscious, originated within his skull, woven on the marvellous electrochemical loom of his brain. The raw materials feeding the brain came both through his five senses and the nerves monitoring his body.

THE SPIRITUAL FACTOR

This view is even held by a large proportion of those who still pay lip service to the religious teachings that there is a non-material factor – the spiritual – capable of influencing and being contacted by human beings. Some believe that their thoughts are their own, and that their dreams, by night or by day, are the products of their mind and brain: their fantasies, their wishful thinking, belong solely to them. If they are surprised or terrified by the events in their dreams, they attribute this to the fact that the dream-producer, the 'master of ceremonies', is their unconscious, that they have had too much to eat for supper, or that they are worried about something. In their dreams, they are like a person at the cinema who views a film he has had no hand in producing. 'What an imagination I have!' they say in self-admiration.

Unfortunately, not all people can believe this to be the case – among them, multiple personality cases, in which a number of distinct characters dispute the possession of one body. In some such individuals, it seems that the original personality has been shattered by one or more traumatic experience and has given rise to 'secondary' personalities. But others, carefully studied by psychiatrists, demonstrate such bizarre features that the possibility of actual invasion by independent personalities, or parts of personalities, has to be seriously considered. If such a theory seems to the man in the street to be a woeful return to the superstitions of the Dark Ages, its proponents would reply that he is simply ignorant of the facts.

During the last 100 years or so, scores of multiple personality cases have been treated and carefully studied by authorities such as Freud, Jung, William James, Morton Prince, Walter F. Prince and others. Many have common features; but it is rash to assume that the same explanation will suffice to cover all of them.

Let us suppose that the personality is a girl. Often she is quiet, reserved, joyless, hyperconscientious. Often she has had a very unhappy upbringing, and is the product of a violent home. She may find herself puzzling over lost stretches of time, the events of which she cannot remember. Strange clothes appear in her wardrobe, and she gradually comes to fear for her sanity. If she consults a psychiatrist, she may be fortunate enough to find one who recognises her condition and encounters one or more secondary personalities that from time to time surface to take control of the body and obliterate the dowdy, everyday personality.

In a number of cases, the major secondary personality turns out to be bright and fun-loving, openly contemptuous of the quiet girl with whom she shares a body. Dislike and contempt of the secondary personality may find an outlet in playing

Dr Walter Franklin Prince, a minister of religion and also a psychologist, above, investigated many cases of multiple personality and of apparent possession by spirits. One of his most celebrated cases was that of Doris Fischer, who had five personalities – one of whom claimed to be a form of guardian spirit.

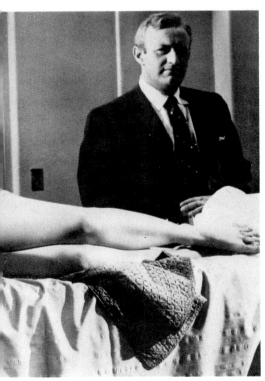

tricks upon the bewildered rival, who has no knowledge of the fun-lover's existence, nor memories of the experiences of the other. On the other hand, the fun-lover is often fully aware of everything the dowdy one experiences when the latter is in control. So different are the two characters that the psychiatrist treating the case knows which personality is in control immediately the girl enters the room – a knowledge due not only to different tastes in fashion but also to an almost physical transformation of the patient's face. Truly, Robert Louis Stevenson displayed remarkable insight into the complexities of the human mind when he wrote *Dr Jekyll and Mr Hyde* in the late 19th century.

ONE BODY, FIVE OCCUPANTS

As many as five or six separate personalities in one body, quite distinct in their beliefs, ethics and mental ages, have been displayed in a number of cases. In that of an American woman, Doris Fischer – studied by Dr Walter F. Prince of Pittsburgh – for instance, there were five personalities: Doris, Margaret, Ariel, Sick Doris and Sleeping Real Doris. Doris was the 'normal' quiet, bewildered personality, while Margaret was the mischievous one who got Doris into trouble. Ariel appeared when Doris was asleep and always claimed to be a spirit who had come to protect her. Sick Doris gave the impression of being a dull, nervous, timid, almost simple-minded person. Sleeping Real Doris seems to have had predominantly the role of guardian of memories: she had no marked separate personality, but could reel off memories of past events, like a living tape-recorder. Dr Prince described her as 'sleeping' because this ability lay dormant most of the time.

Dr Prince and his wife took the sorely troubled girl to stay with them, almost as a daughter; and thanks to the Princes' care and psychiatric treatment, the girl's mental and physical health improved over the next few years. During that time, the complex relationship among the five personalities inhabiting the body of Doris Fischer altered. At first, Margaret had access to the contents of Doris' and Sick Doris' minds, while Ariel was acquainted with the minds of all three. Sometimes, quarrels would occur for control of the body. As time went on, Doris extended her control, as Sick Doris and then Sleeping Real Doris gradually deteriorated and finally disappeared. It was then the turn of Margaret, the sharp, fun-loving one who was slowly to recede until she, too, vanished.

There is a touching and thought-provoking account of the last days of Sick Doris. As she began to disintegrate, she seemed to realise that she was going to disappear. She accompanied Dr Prince on a last walk and left a letter for Margaret. (One of the ways by which each entity communicated with the others was by writing letters when in control. These would be read when the appropriate personality took over the body.) In her letter, Sick Doris instructed Margaret as to what to do with her possessions after her demise and tried to leave her sister-personality some helpful advice.

To the end, Ariel maintained her claim that she was a spirit, sent to look after Doris. In his account, Dr Prince admits that, to him, she was the most

mature and wise of all the personalities and that he had to consider seriously the hypothesis that her claim was in some way true.

The Christine Beauchamp case displayed many similarities to the Doris Fischer case and is quite often confused with the latter, especially since it was treated by another Dr Prince – this time, Dr Morton Prince, a professor at the Tufts Medical School in Boston, USA. Christine Beauchamp was a student, and was approaching a nervous breakdown when she first consulted him. He tried hypnosis, finding that she was a good subject. But to his surprise, a distinct personality emerged – a relaxed, very much calmer version, whom Prince called *B-2* to distinguish her from the first Christine, *B-1*. But more was to follow. *B-2*, under hypnosis, was always rubbing her closed eyes. Prince discovered that it was a third personality, at first called *B-3*, who did the rubbing in an effort to get them open.

B-3 insisted that she had a right to see; and on a subsequent occasion, she at last managed to open Christine's eyes. From then on, she insisted on being known as Sally. She was a bright, mischievous person, not nearly so well-educated as Christine, but exhibiting perfect health in contrast to Christine's debilitated and nervous state. She seemed to hate Christine and claimed that she never slept, but stayed awake while the other personality was asleep. She also continually tormented Christine with practical jokes. According to Dr Prince, Sally went out into the country where she collected in a box some snakes and spiders. She packed them up and addressed the package to Christine, who opened the box in due time and went into screaming hysterics – not surprisingly, since she had a horror of snakes and spiders.

Sally would also force the strait-laced Christine into embarrassing situations in which she would

The transformation of the decent Dr Jekyll into the bestial Mr Hyde is shown, left, in stills from a film version of the classic tale by Robert Louis Stevenson, inset. Hyde was in fact a fragment of a personality – the repressed evil side of Jekyll's nature. In many ways, Stevenson, writing in 1886, anticipated Freud in his view of a potentially destructive, dark side of the mind that threatens the world of reason and light.

have to tell lies. In spite of Dr Prince's efforts, this feud continued until, quite suddenly, a fourth personality, *B-4*, surfaced. *B-4* was a mature, responsible, firm personality who defended the luckless Christine from Sally's torments by giving Sally as good – or as bad – as she gave Christine.

Dr Prince decided that, if he could merge *B-1* and *B-4* and suppress Sally, he might get in tune with the true Christine. Using his hypnotic skills, he attempted to achieve this goal. It is not surprising to learn that Sally resisted to the end, claiming that she had every right to live and enjoy life. But Dr Prince succeeded in producing a more complete personality for Christine, though not quite eliminating Sally. As the years went by, Sally appeared from time to time, as if revisiting old haunts, to indulge herself by playing tricks on Christine.

If a personality under shock can shatter into fragments, so that each fragment is made up of a fraction of all those moods, emotions, beliefs, prejudices, and desires that contribute to the 'normal' person, then – even though, in the Doris Fischer case, Ariel claimed to be a spirit – we can still cling to the belief that no outside influences are at work. But there are a number of cases that, to certain investigators, stretch this hypothesis almost to breaking point.

*In*FOCUS

OF MORE THAN ONE MIND

It has been suggested that population figures for the United States should be increased – so many of its citizens seem to be afflicted, or favoured, by extra personalities.

William Milligan, left, was finally diagnosed as having ten different personalities – one of them, a teenage lesbian.

William Milligan, for instance, was found guilty of raping four young women in Columbus, Ohio, in 1976. He was diagnosed as having ten personalities – of whom the guilty one was an 18-year-old lesbian. One of the psychiatrists who hastened to interview Milligan was Dr Cornelia Wilbur. She had previously treated 'Sybil', the subject of a book and a film, who is said to have had as many as 16 personalities.

But these cases are surely excelled by that of 'Charles' – the pseudonym given by a psychiatrist to what he hoped was the core personality of one of his patients, Eric, who had been found wandering in a daze in Daytona Beach, Florida, in February 1982. Eric immediately 'split' into two selves – 'young Eric' and 'older Eric'.

'Young Eric' told a (fictitious) tale of how he had been brought up by drug dealers, of having been raped, and of having witnessed murders committed by his stepfather.

Further personalities emerged over a period of weeks. These included violent 'Mark', arrogant 'Michael', and blind and mute 'Jeffrey'. Finally, the psychiatrist identified no fewer than 27. The youngest of them was a foetus.

Many of the selves were in conflict and created problems for each other. 'Michael', for example, was athletic and once went on a long jog that left 'Eric' – and all the other occupants of his body – physically aching for days. 'Charles', supposedly the true personality, said afterwards of his existence: 'I've lived through hell. I'm surprised I didn't go crazy.'

FURTHER EXPERIMENTS IN ASTRAL TRAVEL

WHAT HAPPENS WHEN SOMEONE'S 'ASTRAL BODY' VISITS A PLACE DURING AN OUT-OF-THE-BODY EXPERIENCE? PROFESSOR A. J. ELLISON DESCRIBES FURTHER EXPERIMENTS

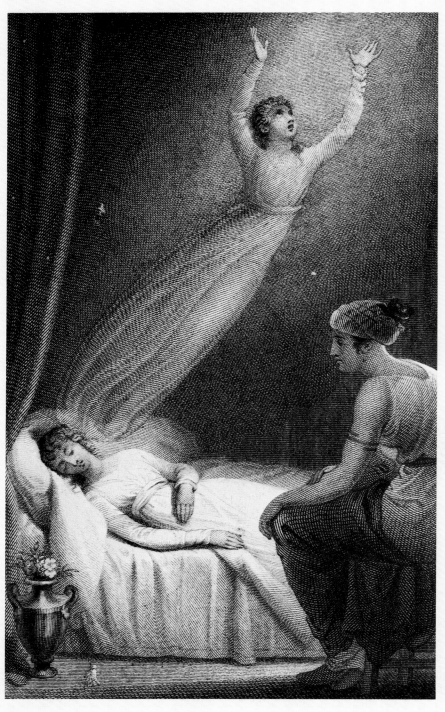

One of the major difficulties in psychical research is how to eliminate the possible intervention of telepathy. The problem is especially acute in the investigation of out-of-the-body experiences (OOBEs). The obvious way to test an OOBE is to ask the person undergoing the experience to 'visit' a place that he or she has never seen when awake, and then to ask for a detailed description of the surroundings, which can later be checked. But it seems that there is no way of knowing whether a real OOBE is involved, or whether the subject could be using clairvoyance to gain such information. Another interesting suggestion has been made: that having an OOBE may act as a trigger, bringing to the surface information that is lying passive in the subject's subconscious. Indeed, it could be that even everyday experiences such as seeing, hearing, touching, smelling and tasting are all mere illusions, and that we in fact sense the physical world by clairvoyance.

To combat this problem, I had built several years ago a box containing some fairly sophisticated electronic circuitry. With the subject of the experiment in an OOBE state, I could – by pressing a button at the front of the machine – make a three-digit random number appear at the back – out of my sight. I would then ask the subject to tell me the number at the back of the machine, and enter the number he or she gave me on another dial at the front of the machine. The machine would tally the numbers on the two dials and note whether or not the subject had been successful in stating the original number correctly. This procedure could be repeated any number of times to give a run of experiments. At the end of a run, the dials could then be set to display the number of successes. (The machine could also indicate how many of the separate digits corresponded on each occasion, if it should be that this information was required.)

The important point about this method is that, since at no time – before, during or after the experiment – are the random numbers in the mind of the experimenter, the influence of telepathy of any kind is thereby ruled out. The next step was to use the box to test a number of subjects who, as previous experiments had shown, were able to have OOBEs when this suggestion was made to them under hypnosis. (It is an ability fairly common among good hypnotic subjects.)

I started with two or three trial runs in which, for speed, I looked at the numbers at the back of the box while the first subject was attempting to tell me what they were. These runs were remarkably successful. So we started a run of 25 tries in which I did not look at the numbers in the window at the back, but used the method described above. Almost at once, the subject seemed to be in difficulty, and said that she was finding it impossible to 'read' the numbers clearly, as they were 'too small'.

The astral body is said to leave the physical body at death, as shown in the illustration by the French artist Corbould, far left. People who experience OOBEs often describe them in terms of a journey undertaken by the 'astral body'; but what actually happens during an OOBE is still the subject of debate.

Professor Arthur Ellison, left, devised a method for investigating the nature of OOBEs. A figure produced by a random number generator appears; the subject of the experiment is then asked to go in his 'astral body' and read the number. The number he sees is recorded on the dial at the front of the machine, and the machine checks whether or not the reading is correct. At no time is the original random number seen in the ordinary sense by anyone. Thus, a successful reading by the subject indicates that his OOBE is not dramatised telepathy.

// My memory of the details seen when still unconscious is still vivid and there is no doubt in my own mind that my vantage point at that moment was detached from my body. **//**

Lyall Watson, The Romeo Error

I suggested that she practise with small numbers set up by a friend at home (and looked at afterwards, for the recording of 'right' or 'wrong'), and asked her to return in a month or two to continue more rigorous experiments using the box. It was no surprise to me, however, when she did not reappear as arranged.

A second hypnosis subject proved even less successful, was unable to read the figures at the back of the box under any conditions, and did not continue the experiments.

BEATING THE ODDS

My third subject was a famous American psychic who came to our laboratory during a visit to Britain and was told about the machine I had developed. He volunteered to try a run immediately – unfortunately, not giving us time to check that the box was in fact functioning properly. He indicated confidently that the numbers would 'just appear' in his mind, and an OOBE experience was not necessary in his particular case. This, of course, raises some interesting questions about the nature of OOBEs. There is certainly plenty of evidence that information can appear in the mind without any particular procedure, such as inducing an OOBE, being necessary. The psychic ran through a series of around 20 'guesses'. At the end, I turned the dial to see how many he had got right, expecting to find a zero score – and, to my astonishment, the window indicated eight.

But the following morning, I decided to investigate further, and did a run myself, and also scored eight. Clearly, there was something wrong. Careful examination indicated a non-visible fault in a microcircuit, resulting in all seven bars of the units digit being illuminated, forming the figure eight. The psychic's score had therefore been due to a misreading. Careful cleaning of the component in question reduced my score on a subsequent run to its usual zero.

The fourth subject to use the box was a famous British psychic. This time, the experiment was

---

P E R S P E C T I V E S

TESTING A VIEWPOINT

Investigators into astral projection have been presented with many different accounts of out-of-the-body experiences by way of evidence that the phenomenon exists, and have also embarked upon scientific experimentation; but the possibility that clairvoyance or telepathy of some kind are involved still remains.

In his book *To Kiss Earth Goodbye*, American artist Ingo Swann tells how, as a small child, he once left his body while on the operating table as the surgeon removed his tonsils, and even saw the scalpel accidentally cut the back of his tongue. He also heard the surgeon swear at his mistake. This ability to leave his body at will continued and was later tested at Stanford University with quite spectacular results. Swann seemed able, for instance, to project himself way beyond this planet and described with considerable accuracy the features of Mercury, right down to the shape of its magnetic field – all this some time before Mariner 10 was able to confirm his descriptions. Researchers found, however, that his description

of Jupiter was nowhere near as detailed and even misinformed in some respects.

Accurate descriptions were also given by Bob Morrell who, when subjected to torture while in the Arizona State Penitentiary, claimed often to have left his body as a direct reaction to such treatment and to have wandered freely outside the jail. Thus he was able to outline to researchers events that occurred in the streets of San Francisco that he could not otherwise possibly have known about. Strangely, once he was no longer subjected to torture, the facility for astral travel promptly disappeared.

In his book *Mysteries*, Colin Wilson, meanwhile, points out potential uses for out-of-the-body experiences. Criminals, for instance, could conceivably use astral travel to help them plan burglaries. He also reminds us of the rather startling claim that occultist Aleister Crowley is said to have used astral travel to commit psychic rape on those women he wanted to possess.

planned and the box carefully checked for correct operation. I did a run or two, and my research assistant did the same. We obtained typically low scores. After allowing plenty of time for the circuitry to warm up and stability to be established, as well as a final check, the visiting psychic made the first run of 20 tries. A score of eight ensued. A check by myself gave another score of eight. Again, there had to be something wrong with the equipment – and, sure enough, careful cleaning of the microcircuit proved necessary. I now did a run, and my research assistant did a run – both resulting in the usual low scores. Everything was working correctly. The psychic did another run – and obtained another score of eight. But when we recleaned the equipment and tried again, we obtained our average low scores. Had the equipment again been at fault? It was impossible to tell.

A sceptical observer might well say that it was mere chance that a fault appeared in the equipment we were using on two occasions when well-known psychics were the subjects of experiment. An experienced psychical researcher, on the other hand, might observe that this kind of thing often happens. It is as though the unconscious mind of the psychic, knowing that a high score was required, achieved

Research conducted at the Psychical Research Foundation in Durham, North Carolina, USA, appears to indicate that animals may be able to detect the presence of astral bodies. Psychic Stuart Blue Harary, below, was able to 'go', while in an OOBE state, and calm a pet kitten, bottom. An objective measure of the kitten's distress was provided by placing it in a box marked into squares, and noting the extent to which it moved.

this by the easiest available method – by using PK on the microcircuit rather than by means of clairvoyance. But no one is currently able to prove this contention: it merely remains a possibility.

Dr Karlis Osis, the Research Officer of the American Society for Psychical Research, conducted some interesting experiments with Alex Tanous to try to determine whether observations during OOBEs are performed with something similar to the human eye. Osis required Tanous, in his OOBE state, to 'look' through the window of a box in which was an optical system superimposing images that gave a certain appearance to normal sight when viewed from a certain point in space. This appearance was, in effect, an illusion – something that did not physically exist – and the experiment

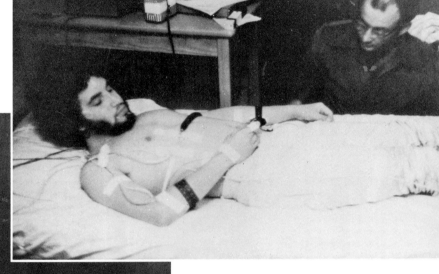

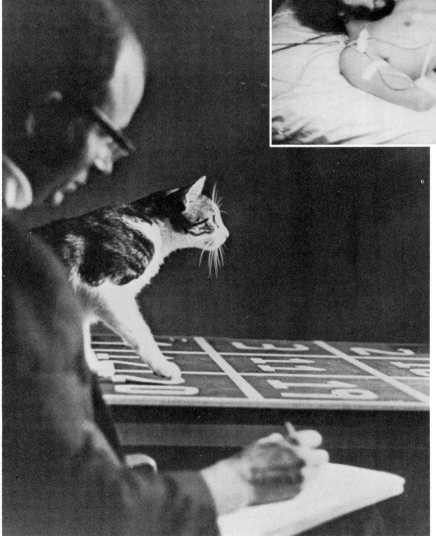

was designed to answer the question of whether OOBEs can be regarded as a kind of dramatised clairvoyance, or whether something (perhaps the 'astral body') actually travels from place to place during an OOBE. Osis claimed that his results indicated some support for the idea of a presence in the physical space in front of the box. There are, however, problems in the interpretation of his results: the limits of clairvoyance are, after all, unknown; and, even though it was possible to choose the target patterns randomly so that no one knew what their appearance to the human eye would be, it may have been possible for the unconscious mind of the subject to deduce the appearance from clairvoyant knowledge of the relative positions of the components in the box, and to dramatise the experience to produce the correct result. Osis claimed that later experiments, in which he placed physical sensors (strain gauges) in front of the window of the optical box, seemed to indicate that some kind of physical object might be there during OOBE observations. There seemed to be a tendency for more 'hits' on the optical targets when the gauges indicated activity.

Further interesting experiments involving psychic Stuart Blue Harary were conducted at America's Psychical Research Foundation in Durham, North Carolina. The aim was to observe

*In*Focus

MISS Z AND THE
HIDDEN NUMBER

The first fully controlled laboratory experiment set up in order to investigate the nature of OOBEs was conducted by Dr Charles Tart, *left,* of the University of California. Dr Tart's subject was a Miss Z, who reported having experienced OOBEs since childhood.

After wiring her up to an electroencephalograph (EEG), Dr Tart then asked Miss Z to put herself into an OOBE state. On a shelf above her head was a slip of paper on which was written a number that had been selected by Dr Tart from mathematical random number tables before the beginning of the experiment. The wires that led from Miss Z's head to the electroencephalograph were designed to be of such a length that she could not physically get up at any point and look at the number on the shelf without causing an obvious interruption in the pattern that appeared on the electroencephalograph print-out.

Nothing significant happened on the first night of the experiment. On the second night, however, Miss Z was successful in experiencing an OOBE, in the course of which she said that she saw a clock on the wall above the shelf – she could not have seen this while lying down – and had 'read' the time as being 3.15 a.m. A check on the electroencephalograph print-out revealed unusual brainwave patterns at that time. On the third night, she had a similar experience.

It was not until the fourth night that she attempted to read the figure on the slip of paper – and, remarkably, did so with complete success. She reported the time of her experience – by the laboratory clock – as somewhere between 5.50 and 6.00 a.m. At 5.57 a.m. on the electroencephalograph tape, it was noted that her brainwave patterns showed a disturbed output. Dr Tart's experiment seemed to show that something paranormal was indeed going on during Miss Z's OOBEs.

" GOING OUT [ASTRAL PROJECTION]

IS A DRAMATIC EXPERIENCE...

THERE IS A VERY POWERFUL

AND VERY RAPID SPIRAL THRUST

OF ENERGY... "

JOHN HERON,

CONFESSIONS OF A JANUS-BRAIN

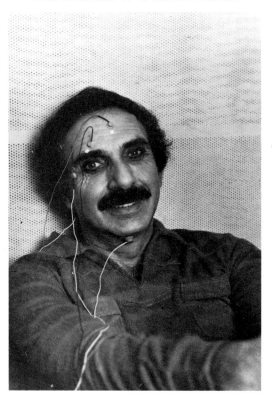

Does anything actually leave the physical body during an OOBE? Dr Karlis Osis, above, of the American Society for Psychical Research, conducted experiments in which he placed strain gauges in front of the site that the subject, psychic Alex Tanous, left – shown wired up to an electroencephalograph as he was during the experiments – is asked to visit.

closely the behaviour of small rodents, snakes and kittens in the presence of an 'astral projection'. The kittens were put in a large, open test box that had been marked into squares. The normal random activity of the kittens could be expressed in terms of the number of squares occupied by a kitten in a given period of time. In normal experimental conditions, the kittens tended to be frightened, cry and move about a great deal. Harary 'went', in an OOBE state, to the kittens' box and tried to calm them. One of the kittens did indeed change in behaviour, its movement and activity both decreasing during the times when Harary was having an OOBE. The other kitten took no notice, however. Later experiments were not very significant, but it appears from the work done by Harary and other researchers that it might be worthwhile to investigate whether animals are actually better than machines as detectors of subjects having OOBEs.

One can reasonably conclude from all this that it may not be meaningful to take subjects' descriptions of their own experiences of OOBEs too literally. Indeed, an OOBE may well be a mental construction, consisting of memories of the physical world, with some information obtained through telepathy or clairvoyance superimposed on it. Eastern scriptures suggest that the 'astral world' to which many people believe we go after death (and which we visit in the 'astral body' during an OOBE) is a 'world of illusion', based perhaps on a combination of our memories of this world and our desires, both conscious and unconscious. As Professor H.H. Price has pointed out, such a world of mental images would be just like the world that is frequently described by mediums and psychics, with all the individual differences one would expect. However, as Professor Price also pointed out, such a 'next world' would not be at all dissimilar from what some philosophers say this world is really like. Perhaps a study of the OOBE would in fact help us towards a better understanding of ourselves, our perceptions and mental processes.

ANIMAL BONDING

IS THE INTELLIGENCE OF OUR PETS INFLUENCED PARANORMALLY BY US? DO WE RECEIVE UNSUSPECTED BENEFITS FROM THEM? THERE IS, IT SEEMS, MUCH TO BE GAINED FROM OUR BONDING WITH ANIMALS

A dog grieves for its dead master in Landseer's The Old Shepherd's Chief Mourner, *above. The bond between dogs and human beings is almost uncanny; and stories of dogs apparently knowing telepathically of their masters' deaths are legion.*

Lord Gardenstone, a Scottish judge of the 18th century, was extremely fond of pigs in general, and one pig in particular. Except when he was actually sitting in his judicial capacity, he was always accompanied by his pet sow, the animal following him about as though it were a dog.

One morning, reports *The Dictionary of National Biography*, a visitor called on Gardenstone at an early hour, well before the time at which the judge normally got up. The visitor was shown into the judge's bedroom, still in semi-darkness, and stumbled over some enormous object 'which gave a terrible grunt'. At this, Lord Gardenstone explained: 'It is just a sow, poor beast, and I laid my breeches on it to keep it warm all night.'

But another source quotes Lord Gardenstone as giving a different explanation as to why, each night, he allowed his pet sow to use his clothes as bedding: it warmed them, and he found it pleasant to don warm clothes on a cold morning.

There is no reason to doubt the truth of either explanation. Doubtless there was some form of exchange transaction from which both parties benefited: the pig was pleased to have a comfortable bed, and the judge was pleased that his breeches were warmed for him. Such exchanges typify the relationship between most pets and their owners; both parties are the gainers. This is provided, of course, the pets are mammals or birds. The exact nature of the benefits received by either party to the transaction is difficult to determine when the pet is something highly exotic – a giant African cockroach, for example.

With a normal household pet, such as a cat or dog, some of the advantages derived from the relationship are obvious. The animal receives warmth, food, care when it is sick, grooming, affection and so on. The owner receives a certain amount of admiration, particularly from a pet dog (which may regard its owner as head of the pack – as, literally, the 'top dog'). He also receives companionship, and – a very important psychological consideration – a sense of being needed, of being the most important factor in the physical and emotional life of a member of another species.

But human beings also gain many less obvious benefits from close relationships with domestic animals. Indeed, the value of pets in soothing, comforting and reassuring people who are unhappy, mentally or physically ill, or under stress, has been demonstrated in numerous scientific studies.

That pet owners are less likely to be anxious or depressed than those without pets is perhaps not surprising. One might say that a pet owner has the welfare of another being beside himself to consider and is therefore less likely to brood upon his own problems. But research has shown that pet ownership may also be of benefit in physical disorders, such as heart disease.

A team of American researchers from the University of Pennsylvania and the Department of Health Science, Brooklyn College, New York, carried out a survey of 92 patients admitted to hospital suffering from coronary disease. Of the sample 92, pets were owned by 53 patients. While these patients were in hospital, most of them expressed concern about the welfare of their pets; and as soon as they were well enough to do so, most of them made daily telephone calls to the friends or relatives looking after the pet. Some of them were so worried about their cat or dog that they regularly had 'conversations' with it on the telephone.

Research has demonstrated that watching pet fish, such as those below, lowers the blood pressure, and thus is probably beneficial to health.

In the 1950s, Karlis Osis, a psychologist, and his assistant Esther Foster, below, investigated the psychic abilities of cats. A cat approached two cups, in one of which there was food. If the cat picked that cup, it was rewarded with the food. If it did not, it received a mild electric shock 'to remind it to use its ESP next time', as Osis put it. He claimed to have obtained statistically significant results, indicating the existence of ESP in the cats.

One might have guessed that worry about their animals would place an additional strain on the coronary patients and make their recovery less likely. But the survey showed that exactly the reverse was the case. Of the 53 pet owners, no less than 50 (94 per cent) were still alive a year after leaving hospital; of the 39 non-owners, only 17 (43 per cent) were surviving at the end of the same period. So marked was the disparity in recovery rates that it was suspected that, by some freak of chance, the group of patients who did not own pets were on average much more seriously ill than the others.

But investigation showed that this was not so and that the improved rate of survival was 'independent of the patient's health status'.

Some indication of the reasons for this remarkable rate of recovery among pet-owning coronary patients may be provided by the results of other American research. A survey found, for instance, that there was a rise in the blood pressure of both men and women when they were engaged in conversation. When, however, the same group of subjects were engaged in petting and 'talking' to dogs, their blood pressure fell. Interestingly enough, a study of children in their homes revealed a similar fall in blood pressure when an animal was present, even if there was no visible interaction between child and pet, such as stroking or vocal communication.

STILL WATERS

Even those pets not biologically capable of interaction with human beings seem to produce the same beneficial effects, as demonstrated by an American experiment involving tropical fish. The subjects were first placed in front of a blank wall and instructed to do nothing but look at the wall; their blood pressure, both systolic (measured when the heart is contracted) and diastolic (when it is expanded), was then measured. The subjects were next placed facing a tankful of tropical fish. As they watched the fish, both systolic and diastolic blood pressure fell. The fall was greatest among those whose blood pressure was high for their age and weight. One particularly interesting feature was that the falls in pressure were quite large, matching those achieved by biofeedback (a technique whereby individuals can learn to monitor certain bodily functions) or by prolonged practice in such relaxation techniques as yogic meditation.

Tropical fish are, of course, not very rewarding to talk to or cuddle. So if watching them can noticeably reduce blood pressure, it can be easily understood that contact with a cat, a dog, or even a parrot, is likely to have the same effect to an even greater degree. A reduction in a coronary patient's blood pressure is, of course, of great importance to his or her health.

Animals that are close to Mankind, and which have regularly been made 'part of the family' – whether they are cats, dogs or something more unusual, such as Lord Gardenstone's sow – seem to sense when their owners are ill or disturbed.

TELEPATHIC CONNECTION

Such a sensitivity to an individual's condition cannot, by its very nature, be tested under laboratory conditions. But many pet owners are convinced that such awareness does indeed exist, and are able to provide much anecdotal evidence of their own experience of it. For example, people who suffer from violent changes of mood have reported that their pet cats and dogs will immediately imitate their behaviour. Sometimes, such awareness of the owner's emotional state is attributed to 'animal telepathy', involving a pet's recognition of the significance of signals that are unconsciously broadcast by the human being, whether by touch, smell or behaviour.

A number of serious researchers into the paranormal have considered that the anecdotal claims of pet owners may have some validity. Thus, J. B. Rhine, perhaps the best known of all parapsychologists, wrote that: 'The number of reported cases [of animal ESP] is large enough to suggest that animals can somehow be affected by circumstances they could not be aware of by any sensory sign and which one would suppose they could hardly understand in human terms.'

Dr Karlis Osis, who for some time worked at Rhine's parapsychological laboratory, claimed statistically significant results from controlled tests of animal ESP that he conducted with cats. But unfortunately, according to Dr Osis, cats are even more difficult experimental subjects than human beings: with a researcher whom they like, results are very good; with ones they dislike, however, they are proportionately poor.

It has to be admitted that claims made by some animal owners regarding their pets' extra-sensory

Sammy, the pet grey squirrel of an Oxfordshire family, is seen, above, making itself a nest using paper tissues and the bowl of a food mixer. Pet owners are familiar with the intelligent adaptations to the human environment made by their animals. But pets do not often have to cope with as many bolts and catches as this chimpanzee does, left, when dealing with an intelligence test.

abilities extend into what most of us would regard as the realms of fantasy. Dogs exhibiting mediumistic powers, cats that seem to be endowed with the gift of psychic healing, horses with visible haloes – all are recorded in the wilder literature of Spiritualism.

But there are rather more firmly-based reports of animals learning to behave remarkably intelligently. To take just one example, pets frequently learn to cope with the door fasteners of new refrigerators so that they can help themselves to food, within minutes of the refrigerator's installation.

Might it even be that the morphogenetic fields posited by biologist Rupert Sheldrake – invisible fields that surround and give shape to life forms, and affect their behaviour – extend across the barriers between species? Could the intelligence of animals perhaps be increasing as a result of contact with their human masters and companions?